HELLO WORLD IT'S ME

A Transformational Journey to freedom.

By Angela Y. Ervin

Foreword By: Dr. Joycelyn Y. Pernell - Henderson

Legacy Books

Legacy Books

Published by Legacy Publishing

Hartford, WI 53027

Copyright: September 28, 2018

ISBN: 978-1-7329316-0-2

Website: www.angelayervin.com

No part of this manual may be reproduced by mimeograph Process of by any other method of duplication unless express Written permission has been granted by

Angela Y. Ervin

Email: info@angelayervin.com

*Unless otherwise indicated all Scripture quotations are Taken from the New International Version of the Bible.

Published by:

Legacy Publishing

Except in the United States of America, this book is sold subject to the condition that it shall not, by way of trade or otherwise, be lent, resold, hired out, or otherwise circulated without the publisher's prior consent in any form of binding or cover other than that which it is published and without similar condition including this condition being impost on the subsequent purchaser.

The scanning, uploading and distribution of this book via the internet or via any other means without the permission of the publish is illegal and punishable by law. Please purchase only authorized electronic editions and do not participate in or encourage electric piracy of copyright materials. Your support of the author's rights is appreciated

To my children, and to my parents

AYE

About the Author

Angela, a mother of three children Javaris, Abigail, Jeremiah and a MIMI (grandmother) of one baby girl named, Paris Chanel. Angela is a CEO, author - speaker transformational, leader and a woman of substance. She has distinguished herself both in the local and international region with a focus on building up other women as bold, confident, successful, professionals, and entrepreneurs, with many years of experience. Angela is dedicated to bringing out the best in every woman.

Angela has established Empowerment Enterprise Network of Women, known as E2NOW - to provide a vehicle for the purposes of empowering, strengthening and promoting women entrepreneurs from the pulpit to the humanitarian stage at such times when entrepreneurship has been considered a man's territory.

We all have our own unique purpose on this planet. As a business professional, Angela plays a significant role in actively getting women aligned with their purpose to achieve their highest potential. She will give you the tools to help you leave your mark on earth.

Foreword

I am humbled that my first-born daughter has asked me to write this forward for this project. It is a very distinct high honor for me that I don't take lightly and will be forever grateful. I believe only when we have successfully passed the test, our heavenly Father will send us back to lead others out. This book is a testimonial bridge for others to walk into their freedom. When tried by fire, we always WIN and come through as PURE GOLD!

Angela, in this new book has become transparent that the entire world can see that – God still uses every broken fragmented piece of our lives for HIS GLORY! The gentleness of her spirit even in writing could be taken to be timidity. However, after reading this book, you will come away knowing this is a Strong Phoenix Woman of Godly character, dignity, wisdom and compassion for others.

This book gives a 21 - day plan to redemption and freedom from almost anything that would try to mask us. I believe this book will also change the trajectory of the life of everyone that reads and commits to following the 21 - day plan. This is written for very easy reading, but also boldly stresses so many critical elements that can be used as a catalyst to place one on the correct path to walk. The reader will come away seeing themselves the same way God See's US.

This is a short list of nuggets that I gain while reading: raising Godly seed; allowing God to select our spouse; walking out of the strangling pit of un-forgiveness; dispelling the spirit of rejection and loving ourselves as Christ has also loved us. I believe every household needs to get a copy of this book for themselves and complete the 21-day strategic plan many times. It is a truth, - after 21 days of consistently doing anything, it should become a habit.

Angela, you are a "Victor" and not a victim. My prayer for you, continue is to seek God's face; continue to allow him to mold you into the prolific writer that even in the heavenlies your name is applauded! You are a Very Rare Jewel in this earth, being used for HIS KINGDOM!

My prayer for all as you read and apply these truths, you will be blessed as I have while gleaning every treasured gem from – HELLO WORLD – IT'S ME!!

Dr. Joycelyn Y. Pernell-Henderson

Founder: Living by Precepts Ministries - Hartford WI

Contents

About the Author 4
Foreword 5
Introduction 9
Session I - Take Your Personal Power Back 11

Day 1 - Impacting My World 12
Day 2 - Divorce Timidity 15
Day 3 - Your Words Frame Your Reality 19
Day 4 - Master The Art of Timing 22
Day 5 - Discipline 25
Day 6 - Self - Love is Ta-Boo 28
Day 7 - Inner Transformation 32

Session II - Free My Soul 35
Day 8 - Overcoming Adultery 36
Day 9 - Forgive -Me-Not 40
Day 10 - Overcoming Rape 43
Day 11 - The Drop - Overcoming Miscarriage 47
Day 12 - O' Tamar – Overcoming Molestation 51
Day 13 - A Sound Mind! 57
Day 14 - Love and Marriage Then Divorce! 60

Session III - I AM Coming OUT..74
Day 15..75
Rejection Bounce..75
Day 16 - I Am Every Woman 83
Day 17 - Free My Soul 86
Day 18 - No One Else Looks Like Me 89
Day 19 - Being Broke Is Not a Joke. 92
Day 20 - Caught In A Net 97
Day 21 - Finding My Home - less. 102

Session V - Conclusion..115
Bonus 117
Day 22 - Think Yourself Rich 118
Quotes 122
Appendix 125

Introduction

The purpose of this journal is to give you, the reader, a 21 - day guide to awaking each day to the world of your dreams! For one whole year, I took time to develop and allowed God to re-create myself to be used for the Kingdom. I will show how you can also do the same, in just 21 days. The process of tearing down and rebuilding was painful yet vital to where I saw myself going. Each day, I focused on transforming, developing and strengthening something different until I saw the results I wanted. This book is my personal experience during this process, and someone's answered prayer.

Some might say, why 21 days and not 30 days? I've chosen 21 days as it is meant for you to repeat the process until you experience a breakthrough. It is said, anything done for 21 days becomes a habit. Trust me, living a transformed life is a habit you want to continue doing throughout your life as you evolve into the woman you were always destined to be. Twenty - one days is not the conclusion, it is an opportunity to mentally modify (measure your skills to bring about an impact) in your thought process of who you are and what you are now... for you to live out loud these strategies written, and when needed reread them again.

Here's my journey and story. As that lady rising as a Phoenix from the ashes of shattered dreams; a story of struggles, hardship and triumphant. Anyone can deal with defeat, but only the strong will experience victory. I am here to show you how you can win always!

Session I

Take Your Personal Power Back

Day 1

Hello World It's me _____.

Impacting My World

Make your presence known; the world shall feel the impact of who you are. You have come out of obscurity into prominence, permanently for this time right now. You are not a day late nor minute early. You are right on schedule of your course. So, shall you run the race given to you long before your mother embraced you. (Jeremiah 1: 5) Though your journey has been tough, you are not afraid to let the world see your scars. Your scars tell a story of the life that tried to break you, beat you, and destroy you. But because the warrior in you knows no defeat, every attempt against you, failed. Giving up was never an option; your Being knows no defeat. You, were not made for it, you were made to be an overcomer. The school of hard knocks taught you to learn from your mistakes.

Devote This Day To Your Success

Set realistic goals, do not make excuses. Stay focus and you will not lose track. From this day onward, harness your confidence hitting the ground running. You are not waiting for the right time. You must declare 'I am here in the right time the earth is waiting for me and I will not let her wait any longer. I will make the most of my time while preparing for what I asked. When the time is right, all of the elements will fall into place. You may not have all of the right answers, but you will keep moving anyway, you shall not lose rhythm. You will be connecting the dots to see the bigger picture; looking at things in a "past, present, and future" context to receive favorable results.'

Your destiny shall be clear, and you will be committed to what you are working towards, going the extra miles while superseding your exceptions. Alertness and awareness breed success the diligent shall rule the lazy. (Proverbs 12:24) Your destiny demands that you listen to what is being said, most importantly what is not constantly hone in on feedback about yourself and your field of impact.

I decree that you shall persevere, never giving up. Will you fall? Yes, however with God within you, you develop a willingness to get back up and try again working through the challenges you will face along your journey. Make every effort to remain humble never allowing success to come with an ego; holding yourself accountable at all times.

Plan All the Way To The End

The ending is everything. Taking account all the possible consequences, obstacles, and twist of fortunes that might reverse your hard work. Give the glory to God and to others who helped you along the way. By planning to the end, you will not be overwhelmed by circumstances and you will know when to stop when you have met your desired goal. Gently guide wealth to appropriate places and to those that are to help you.

Determine the future by thinking far ahead. Success is to be measured not so much by the position that one has reached in life, but by the obstacles which she or he has overcome.

Response:

1. Is your destiny clear?
2. Are you ready to make an impact?
3. Do you understand why you are in the earth?

Declaration:

I will never doubt myself again nor my capability to accomplish and achieve my goals and dreams. I am a go-getter, a doer, and not lazy. I will take responsibility for my life and fulfill my purpose.

Day 2

Hello World It's me_____.

Divorce Timidity

Courage does not desolate itself in confidence, it displays itself in fear. Avoid being afraid of men and what they can do to you.

God Has Not Given Us A Spirit Of Fear But One Of Power. (2 Timothy 1:7)

Stop being afraid of what could go wrong and remember all that can and shall go right. You must keep a positive outlook on life. Your world is framed by your inner reality.

Every new season (winter, spring, summer, fall), there are things that God wants to bring to you. Winter causes the trees to address its roots. Your winter is for you not for anyone else. It is your time of turning in to address your core values and revisiting your character. Use lessons of past experiences for the next season you will enter.

The time is never wasted. God and you economizes every opportunity, (good bad or indifferent), given to you for your advancement and the success of your future self. Your future self need you to be focused, sharp, witty, strong, courageous, and fierce.

What Is Woman

Growing up I thought I had what being woman figured out. All the women around me or at least those I looked up too had very nice homes, had good jobs, beautiful families and were involved in their community. Their plates were completely filled. Looking back, I don't know how they did it. As I am writing this, my three children are adults. I am grateful for the days I come home to only take care of myself. Being a woman in this day and age means being an agent for change. I stand on the brilliant shoulders of the women who have went before me.

Every day I try to always be aware of what they have afforded me and I am grateful for the tools given. I will call for women to used whatever tools they have been given whether they are entrepreneurs, stay at home mom, and in the professional arena. To speak up, shout out and forge ahead. What will you tell your daughters and sons? How will you help them?

Being a woman to me is being the God expression in earth. We are not just simple people, we have complexity. The force behind every woman is the pure life essence of God. We are not the average women.

We are light in darkness, (Ephesians 5:7-14) love where there is hate, and the mother of all living things. As eternal beings, we have power to be what we want to be, to get what we desire. To accomplish whatever you are striving for, abides within you and I. We are making head ways in every arena; professionals, entrepreneurs, and domestic. We are royalty, chosen before the beginning of time. Everyone of us. We have no time to worry about the mundane things. We, are too busy executing the part of our purpose were destined for which were created.

But You Are A Chosen People, A Royal Priesthood. (1 Peter 2: 9b)

Enter Action With Boldness

Time and chance happen to all of us. Chance is an opportunity. However, if you are unsure of a course of action, do not attempt it. Your doubts and hesitations will infect your execution. Timidity is dangerous. Better to enter with boldness. Any mistakes you commit through audacity are easily corrected with more audacity. Be fearless and courageous. Everyone admires the bold; no one humors the timid.

Say out aloud "I shall not miss my chance by timidly misjudging opportunities. No negative external force towards me, shall prevail against me. With proactive words, I cleanse my lens to see things as they are and I have a "chance" to upload a plan of purpose that already has my genetic code.

Once you learned how to defeat self-sabotaging thoughts, you will never be schemed out of opportunities again that you don't feel you are "ready" for due to fear. God shall shift your mental construct and your life forever.

Response:

When your mind and heart agree on anything it shall be done for you. There is a force unleashed to bring from the invisible to the visible. When there is an absence of doubt and a release of faith from your heart.

Declaration:

My mind is free of all thoughts of fear, timidity, and incapacity. I am bold, free, and courageous.

Day 3

Hello World It's Me _____.

Your Words Frame Your Reality

There is a strategy for everything, everything in the world fits into an equation. From the beginning God used the strategy of the "spoken" word and everything that exists does so, because of seed potential of those words. (Genesis 1:1) God has given you a strategy, to live out of your place of dominion on earth. Did you know? Words are our power source; it is the open door to the formless to the form worlds of vibrations. Pertaining to the expression of sound. Every word that goes forth receives its specific character from the power faculty.

A principle taken from (John 6:63) of the Bible says "The words that I have spoken unto you are spirit, and are life," it is meant that through the spoken word is conveyed an inner spiritual quickening quality that would enter the mind of the recipient and awaken the inactive spirit and life. It will lay dormant until you understand the power of the word (seed) within you, thereby discovering the keys to writing your best life.

Each of us have our own journey to walk out, no one else can do it for us. How do we walk out our journey? The lower realm of thinking must be swallowed up with the higher realm of thinking. You cannot live life trying to fix things up. When we live out of a trouble awareness, always trying to control, manipulate, and fix things, it brings us a lot of hurt and a lot of confusion. We must let go of human reasoning. Walk in the spirit, pray and meditate then shall you reconcile your mind with the mind of God. (2 Corinthians 5:20)

It is not a someday experience, you can live out this realm Now. That which brings you pain will be swallowed up and bring you joy. If you want to experience all that God has for you, you must set your affections on things above and not on things that are beneath you. (Colossians 3:2)

You have a seed (word), that seed requires pressure and pressure requires heat. The higher the pressure, the higher the temperature and the higher the heat content. There is a saying that "if you can't take the heat get out of the kitchen."

Today like never before, be determined not to be afraid of opposition. Opposition, is the necessary ingredient in your life that puts the bread on your table. If you want fruit that remain, then you should exercise speaking good when contrary tempts you. It is not what is without a man that defiles him it is what within that defiles a man. (Mathews 15:11) What you allow in your awareness is that which defiles you when temptation comes.

Response:

I must look at things through the eyes of Spirit rather than the natural. I must hear things through the eye of the Spirit rather than in the natural.

Declaration:

Today, commit to using words wisely, with the understanding that all of heaven and earth will pass away but my words will forever remain looking for an opportune time to manifest. Every word I utter makes an imprint on the earth. (Luke 21:33)

Day 4

Hello World It's Me _____.

Master the Art of Timing

Time and chance is given to us all. Time is a human invention and acts as a barrier to a broader conception of creative processes. These are the days you must employ your time wisely in order to harness creativity. What is creativity? The use of the imagination or original ideas, especially in the production of an artistic work. On this 4th day, focus on your creativity. Creativity is bringing something new into form such as a music composition, a book, a cake design, a comedic act or a physical object such as an invention, or a painting. What do you want to create, build, design, begin, or start? If you had all of the money, who would you bless? What issues would you heal? What problems would you solve? Start thinking in this direction and use your abundance to fund global answers.

Exercise Patience

Never seem to be in a hurry – hurrying displays a lack of control over yourself, and over time. Always seem patient as if you already know that everything is going to work in your favor. Others often see impatient people as arrogant, insensitive, and impulsive. They can be viewed as poor decision makers, because they make quick judgments or interrupt other while communicating. Some people will even avoid impatient people, because of their poor people skills and bad tempers.

Become a private eye of the right moment - discern the spirit of the times, the trends that will move you into power. (1 Chronicles 12:32) Learning to navigate all the waiting and unknowns and days of messiness can overwhelm, discourage and frustrate any one of us. You must be patience until the time is ripe, and make your move when things are coming to fruition.

Exercise:

Choose to live life by these 3 simple rules:

1. If you do not ASK, the answer will always be NO.
2. If you do not GO after what you want, you will never have it.
3. If you do not STEP FORWARD, you will always be in the SAME PLACE.

Today, commit to the fulfillment of your purpose. Commit to developing your strengths, power, and mastery. They are not to be exercised on other people but on yourself. "He that ruleth his spirit, **is more powerful** than he that taketh a city." (Proverbs 16:32)… Say OUT LOUD: I CAN DO THIS. You make a choice to take a chance to change your life forever. Converse your focus by keeping your mind concentrated on your strongest points.

You will gain more by finding a gold mine and digging in it deeper, than concentrating with a shallow mind to another intensity every time. When looking for a source of power to elevate you, find the one key source, that field will continue to yield increase every time.

Response:

Intentionally set your mind and heart to agree on anything it shall be done for you.

What You Decide Shall Be Done. (Job 22:28)

When my response is absent of doubt I release faith, the force necessary to bring fulfillment.

Declaration:

I let go of worn-out conditions and worn-out things. Divine order is established in my mind, body and affairs.

Behold, I Make All Things New. (Isaiah 43:18)

Day 5

Hello World It's Me _____.

Discipline

Women who will not take the time to discipline themselves to get what they desire; will never win. To be disciplined is to train yourself to obey a certain code of behavior using strict rules.

Without discipline and hard work, it's almost impossible to be at the "top" in anything. Discipline is a key principle. I often advise my children who desire to have good health, peace with men and happiness within, to have discipline, order and structure in their life. It may be hard when your friends are hanging out or the idea of "sleeping – in" versus going to the gym. However, studies show that people with discipline are happier and healthier.

Studies also show that people who have self-control spend less time debating whether or not to indulge in behaviors that are detrimental to their health and happiness. They don't let impulses or feelings dictate their choices. Instead, they make level-headed decisions. As a result, they tend to feel more satisfied with their lives.

Exercise:

Acknowledge your 5 major shortcomings.

1. _____
2. _____
3. _____
4. _____
5. _____

Today, commit to disciplining any part of your life that you have allowed to get out of control. Say out loud, I will not be overcome by weakness; be it chips, snacks, candy, technology or illicit sex… Yield not to temptation, but set clear goals and have a plan of execution.

Do Not Offer Any Part Of Yourself To Sin As An Instrument Of Wickedness. (Romans 6:13)

Build yourself - discipline by creating new habits and keeping them simple, discipline is not genetic, it is learned, just like any other skills you must practice daily until you have mastered it.

Change your perception regarding your willpower. According to a study by Stanford University, the amount of willpower a person has is predetermined by their beliefs. If you believe you have a limited amount of willpower, you probably won't surpass those limits.

Response:

You will remember to give yourself a backup plan, reward yourself and forgive yourself.

Declaration:

My sensory appetite no longer clogs the clarity of my judgment. The cleaning life of spirit quickens and cleanses my taste, and I eat and drink only what my body requires. I have made a choice to take a chance to change my life forever.

Day 6

Hello World It's Me _____.

Self - Love Is Ta-Boo

We live in a society of people who love everyone else except themselves. We praise everyone for achieving success, while, being critical about ourselves. In some ethnicities it is conveyed daily if not weekly how bad of a tyrant we are as humans. How a loving God will punish us to a never-ending inferno of hell, in a deep bottomless pit, if we did not follow His strict rules. Rarely is positive affirmation used to build or repair what's torn down. We are all God's sons in whom God is well pleased. (Matthew 3:17) No matter what we've done, God still loves us and calls us 'Son'. Son has a Greek meaning which is belonging to. You and I belong to God. Nothing can change that.

You cannot effectively love anyone else until you first love everything that means anything about yourself. We as a human race have to fall in love with loving ourselves and cease with the self-rejection, self-abandonment, and self-inflicting wounds. Women wound themselves more than men; we take things like divorce harder than most men. Instead of getting an understanding that the perpetrator has inner issues that need to be addressed. We personalize it as rejection until we become bitter and resentful. Just because someone did not notice your value, doesn't mean that you do not have any. You notice it! Parked cars are the only objects that need validation. You must exercise your power; it is not the responsibility of anyone to validate you.

We Have Latent Power To Swing Open All The Doors Of Mind and Body

When you feel vital and energetic, your voice is strong, vibrant and brilliant. When you are sorrowful, your body weakens, and your voice betrays its lack by its mournful intonation. Your mouth is closer to your ears than that of anyone outside you. No external forces will have any greater power than your internal voice. A major problem I've noticed is a lack of understanding of the relationship God has with humanity.

You cannot get a right understanding of the relationship that God has with you until you set clearly before yourself the character of God. So long as you think of God in terms of personality, you fail to understand the relationship existing between man and God. Dismiss the thought that God is a man, or even a man exalted far above human characteristics. God is Spirit, created other spirits (mankind) in likeness and image, reflective in nature.

My Own Personal Experiences Allowed Me To Realize I Wasn't Reflecting The Nature Of God

My divorce was the awakening I needed to stop rejecting, self-sabotaging and abusing myself. It was the process of elimination, of what my ex thought and the toxic mindset. I came into realization that personally there was nothing wrong with me. I had to accept that. Accepting was the hard part when all I'd heard was contrary to my new belief. It wasn't until that harsh period of the divorce, I began to understand who and what I was and begin to love the girl who starred back to me in the mirror at me. I deeply love her from inside out.

Nothing can change that feeling I get when I look at myself in the mirror. No outward validation, no rejection, no job, no amount of money, no man. I love the person I am today and evolving into being. I have developed myself gradually from within myself. The transforming of my mindset, habits, daily routine, associations, actions, and life was so painful but was so necessary for me to evolve.

Small Voice

Your ears are no longer stopped by the sensitiveness and willfullness of the little self. The little self is not hard to identity. It seeks its own way, easily offended, selfish, proud, and in all ways, places the emphasis on temporal things. The little self wants to be the master. You must not make it the master. You must say, not my will but thine will be done.

Yet Not My Will, But Yours Be Done. (Luke 22:42b)

Then the cleansing life of Spirit will purify your heart and bathe you in the ocean of life. Trust the "still small voice" within your soul. When He speaks do not cut your wrist, do not drink yourself away. You don't have to binge eat, then vomit later, put down those drugs, do not abuse your body with illicit sex, and over indulging in anything that is not good.

On the contrary, if the voice within you is saying to you "you are ugly and no one will love you, no one wants you", recognize this is a lie. Remember someone manipulated that voice and instilled that voice within you when you were young. Parents let us be mindful that the way we speak to our children becomes their inner voice. If you are hearing that manipulated voice…with your own voice, kill it, destroy its power to influence you!

Exercise:

Ask yourself three questions

1. What or who damaged me?
2. What is stopping me from loving me?
3. Why do you treat yourself the way you do?

Response:

You are not damaged goods…something that was expected to be good, but after careful examination discovered wasn't. YOU ARE GOOD and have always been good.

Declaration:

Starting now, I will tell myself the things I've been waiting to hear as validation from someone else. I AM what I say I AM. I SHALL be what I AM declare I SHALL be.

And God Said Unto Moses, I AM THAT I AM. (Exodus 3:14b)

Day 7

Hello World It's Me _____.

Inner Transformation

For years, I covered my face as many women do, in make-up. Consciously, I felt prettier. I was unaware I masked my personality behind make-up. I am not against make-up. I still wear cosmetics during my designated "me" time, when I am hanging out with friends or speaking at an event. I shall when I make my official guest appearance on a television show.

However, I do not wear make-up to mask a persona that hides my deepest thoughts, feelings and presents a polished, controlled face to the world. Phycologist says masking is a process in which individuals change or "mask" their natural personality to conform to social pressures, abuse, and/or harassment. An individual may not even know he or she is wearing a mask because it is a behavior that can take many forms.

Transformation

Unlike masking, transformation is a thorough or dramatic change in form or appearance. It is a choice of mankind declaring his own personal freedom. The truest indication you are free is when you no longer desire to judge anything, or any person. You see everything including self through the lens of love as created by God. Love is like the sun in one respect, for it is only when it shines out from itself to others that it can be said to be performing its true function.

Declare Your Freedom

But man can never be free until he declares his freedom. Jesus said, "I am from above" (John 8:23). It is the prerogative of every man to make this declaration and thereby rise above the psychism of mortal thought. Then do not fear to develop your power and mastery. They are not to be exercised on other people but on yourself.

"He That Ruleth His Spirit, Is More Powerful Than He That Taketh A City (Proverbs 16:32b)

Today men are striving to acquire power through money, legislation, and man-made government, and falling short because they have not mastered themselves.

It's Time To Re-Create Yourself

When it comes to transformation no man can do any real transforming without a certain realization of spiritual power, dominion, mastery. Do not accept the roles that society places on you. Re-create yourself by forging a new identity, one that commands attention. Be the master of your own image rather than letting others define it for you. Incorporate dramatic devices into your life and action – your power will enhance and your character will seem larger than life.

Response:

You will be mindful of your thoughts. A random thought from the original pattern can throw your life and destiny into disarray if not properly discerned and halted.

Declaration:

My thoughts are proceeding along an orderly path in accordance to God's word.

My Steps Are Ordered Of The Lord. (Proverbs 37:23b)

Session II

Free My Soul

Day 8

Hello World It's Me _____ .

Overcoming Adultery

Adultery is one of the worst things that can happen to a marriage and violates everything you've built with your partner in such a painful way. Many of you who have been a victim of an adulterous affair did not see it coming. You were blindsided, and before you could even process what was happening, you were involved emotionally, physically or both with a person other than our spouse. For me, infidelity felt like the death. The fatal blow was that my ex-husband thought while married to me, that he'd finally found the person that God had intended for him to be with all along.

The thought of filling in "space" until she showed up was heart-wrenching. Once he was convinced that he married me, the "wrong" person, divorce was inevitable. As heartbreaking as it was, I knew I must move on. Emotionally I could not see the light behind the cloud. Most days, I spent rehearsing what I could have done differently to prevent this nightmare from occurring. I realized it was nothing that I did, it was his own personal choice. Some might say he was deceived by the 'devil'. Was it really the 'devil'? Instead of taking ownership for the wrong we've done, we tend to place blame, on a powerless external force. The 'devil' has no power, except for the power we give with our mind. My ex-husband, made a choice with only himself in mind. His choice changed the trajectory of our entire family. His mind was so twisted at that time, he thought and mentioned to our children that I was never his wife. Oddly, I can say, I agree. Our souls were never connected. We weren't vibrating on the same frequency. Together, but not happily married. I spent the final days of our separation: crying, praying, fasting and some nights awake.

Then A Light Bulb Came On:

Why was I decrying to God to restore a marriage with someone who obviously did not ever want nor love me. That very moment I snapped out of the pit of feeling sorry for myself. It was the "aha" moment I needed to transform myself, into a better version of me. I began to dig deep in the transformation process of studying the mind and what causes it to be dis-eased.

At this point, I was mentally dis-eased, and disconnected from my real self. It was then I discovered we shape our reality and frame our future, with negative and positive thoughts about ourselves. We unconsciously shape who we are by the thoughts we produce. Producing wrong thoughts gives us painful results. The mind is the greatest motherboard, it stores for future usage everything that is input into it. Our minds at times requires a reboot in order to operate properly.

Medical authorities tell us that certain organs of the body are self-renewing. That it is a puzzle to them how these parts never wear out. If you had a sewing machine that constantly replaced the little particles worn away by friction, would that machine ever be destroyed? A healthy, man's body has this power of replacing worn parts, and when it is in harmony, it never wears out. This harmony refers to self-adjustment to the law of being, to the law of divine nature, and to the law of God.

It does not matter what you call this fundamental principle underlying all life: the important thing is to understand it, and to put yourself in harmony with it. Changing your thoughts from feeling sorry for yourself, remove self-pity, cease from worry, and self-rejection. Transform your mind, body, and spirit into divine harmony with God. On Gods plan, will, purpose, and intent of life. Changing your thoughts changes your reality.

Response:

You aren't a player piano… You will not play sad pieces, funeral marches, monotones, chants and sing a long (misery loves company). (Proverbs 15:15) You shall throw those away and put in lively happy melodies. They will give you a complete change of spirit… and soon you'll forget all your woes, troubles and build up a new mental condition.

Declaration:

I commit to governing my thoughts. Having the right thought and using the right words. Help me to regain the knowledge of the kingdom within me.

The Kingdom Of God Is Within. (Luke 17:21b)

Day 9

Hello World It's Me _____.

Forgive-Me-Not

Forgiving was hard for me. I could hold a grudge as long as a whale could hold its breath under water. I suffered many years from the disease, of unforgiveness. Merriam Webster describes unforgiveness as: unwilling or unable to forgive. Unforgiveness is classified in medical books as a disease. According to Dr. Steven Sandiford, chief of surgery at the Cancer Treatment Centers of America, refusing to forgive makes people sick and keeps them that way. Of all cancer patients, 61 percent have forgiveness issues. And more than half of this percentage are severe cases.

According to research by Dr. Michael Barry, a Pastor and the author of the book, The Forgiveness Project, states "Harboring these negative emotions, anger and hatred, creates a state of chronic anxiety." If left undealt, unforgiveness will cause dis-ease in the body and even death.

It's time to free your soul. Rid your body, mind of this unwanted dis-ease.

Letting Go

At the time it seemed like God dealt me an unfair hand. Hurt by people I put my trust in only to have to now forgive those same people who act like they hadn't done anything wrong. I got pain, and they got freedom without having to pay for the pain they caused. They've moved on, and I was stuck to deal with what happened.

It took several years, but I realize that forgiveness was for me and not for them. The person who hurt me was not my problem, they were the symptom to an underlying issue. Find the lie and you solve not only your problem but that of the world. Since I have chosen to forgive, everyone. I am happier, free without all of the poison and toxin in my body. The doors are swinging wide open in my favor. There is nothing blocking the blessings from locating me.

To Prove A Point

Forgiveness also releases the other person from the debt. You must move out of the way so God can do what only He can do. If you are in the way—trying to take revenge or take control of the situation yourself—God has no obligation to deal with that person. In the midst of forgiving the people who hurt you, you must also forgive yourself. Forgiveness really means giving up something. You have to give up the idea of wanting God to punish another. Or the desire to want other people who may not know them as you know them, to see who they truly represent. Give up on proving a point. When you forgive yourself, you cease doing the things that you should not do.

Do Not Take Revenge, My Dear Friends. (Romans 12:19b)

It is through forgiveness that true spiritual healing is accomplished. Forgiveness removes errors of the mind, and bodily harmony results in consonance with divine law.

Response:

You always become negative, soft, plastic, to that objective unto which you often give your inner eye. Yield to God's pruning. He makes your heart soft, so that you can forgive others as you have already been forgiven.

Declaration:

I forgive everyone, and everyone forgives me. The gates swing open for my good. I speak forth my healing which includes the whole-man, my body, my environment, my circumstances as well as my Spirit.

I Tell You, Not Seven Times, But Seventy-Seven Times. (Matthew 18:22b)

Day 10

Hello World It's Me _____.

Overcoming Rape

According to the National Statistic… one in four women and one in six men will be sexually assaulted in their lifetime. One in six women and one in thirty-three men will experience attempted or completed rape in their lifetime. In eight out of ten rape cases, the victim knows the perpetrator. Nearly six out of ten sexual assaults occur in the victim's home or the home of a friend, relative, or neighbor.

Date rape is a fast-growing phenomenon in Pubs and Nightclubs, the essential idea is to spike a target's drink with a sedative drug, usually GHB or Rohypnol, and wait for them to become affected and semi-unconscious. At this point, the perpetrator offers to help the virtually incapacitated victim home, or to a taxi, obviously, nobody will be suspicious as the victim appears simply to be heavily inebriated. Having taken the victim to a secluded spot, the perpetrator proceeds to rape them. The effect of the drug or drugs ensures they can't offer any resistance or remember the experience/assailant. Due to the nature of the crime, in up to 80% of date rapes, the victim knows the rapist well, which raises the question why? Why would someone open up to anyone, in order to have them take something so scared away from them?

I Used To Wonder Why

I wasn't walking down a street in thigh high boots, and I also wasn't at some stripper club. I was at my 'apartment' when a ministerial and work colleague (to protect his legal name, I will call him John Doe) did the unspeakable. I had just purchased my first vehicle. A day that I should have been proud turned into a horrifying experience.

I was wearing leggings and a cute shirt, still my go-to comfy clothes. John Doe's purpose for coming was the drop off paperwork that I mistakenly left at the dealership. It was still early in the day, so I thought what the heck, let him bring the paperwork and leave. John Doe came in and insisted there was something that I did not fill out and needed to complete in order for me to take full possession of the car. Not long after John Doe was there, he began to rub his hand on my hand, and I insisted that he should stop and let's finish with the paperwork so that he could go home to his wife, and I can take care of my three-year-old child. With completed paperwork in hand, I walked John Doe to the door, he grabbed me firmly and would not let me go. The more I refused, the tighter he gripped.

Out of fear, I laughed. He took me, he entered me against my will, and I struggled, and I resisted. I pushed against him, and I didn't want any of it, but he still pushed against me, raping me.

I Could Have Screamed

I should have screamed. I stayed silent, still berating myself for letting him come in. The fear of my child hearing and witnessing was more important than the violation that was taking place against my body. In the two, five, ten minutes I made a huge mistake. I am forever sorry for. I was raped.

I was taken against my will. After I said no. After I struggled and he held me down against my will. He raped me. And I let him. I made myself go limp, and he still pushed against me.

I huddled on my couch where it happened and cried. I later called a friend who took me to the emergency room where I was given a rape kit, and a police report was filed, and he was later apprehended.

Avenged

Never before has the issue of sexual assault against women seemed so ubiquitous. The Bible is not silent about rape. The accounts of sexual assault against women are heartbreaking, even gruesome. But they are not brushed under a rug or hushed up. In fact, of the three accounts describing a woman who was sexually assaulted, each of them precipitated civil war. Tamar, the account I will discuss; was raped by her half-brother, Amnon, her brother Absalom killed him, and incited a rebellion against his father, King David (2 Samuel 13). Rape was neither covered up nor ignored. Instead, it was answered and avenged. It was such a cultural convulsion that it was answered with outrage and further violence. The cases of rape in Scripture tell us something about the cases of rape we are hearing today: These women must be heard and they must be protected.

Condemnation

Condemnation, is one of the pits that rape victims have to battle. It does not matter what you were wearing or how you smelled. You did not provoke the assault. You were violated, against your will. I encourage every person who has been raped; seek help immediately, find a counselor and focus on your faith in God.

Response:

You are a survivor, whole…whole means all - inclusive of everything, emotionally, physiologically and physically.

Declaration:

The pain of my trauma is removed from my memory. I did not LET this crime happen to me! I did not deserve it and it was NOT my fault! This criminal is a predator, he knew exactly what he was doing, he has done it before and hopeful will not do it again. From this day forward I will no longer, blame myself for the incident. I didn't let him rape me. I was violated. I am not a victim but a victorious overcomer through God.

In All Things We Are More Than Conquers (Romans 8:37b)

Day 11

Hello World It's Me _____.

The Drop - Overcoming Miscarriage

First of all, I am so sorry that you've experienced a loss that has brought you to this day. I and so many women in similar situations all over the world grieve with you and want to remind you that no matter how you feel, the truth is that this is not your fault. Experiencing a pregnancy loss at any stage means that you are probably feeling more sadness than you ever thought possible. Having a miscarriage can be very difficult. The emotional impact usually takes longer to heal than the physical recovery does. Allowing yourself to grieve the loss can help you come to accept it over time.

Facing The World After A Miscarriage Can Be Tough

Take all the time you need to heal. You might grieve longer than you expect. Remembering my own miscarriage thinking that once a few weeks had passed, I should have been over it by then. I felt embarrassed that I was making too big a deal about it. I kept reading that there is no timeline for grief, and everyone heals differently. I couldn't help feeling like I was going beyond the scope of "normal" and that I would be judged for it. Now looking back, I can see how deeply the loss affected me, and how silly it was to expect to be over it so quickly.

Take As Long As You Need

It's ok to ride out the waves of grief – some days are good some days are bad. Some days you may seem good, and then you are suddenly "triggered" and you may melt a little. I wish I had not spent any energy worrying, if I was grieving too much. I could have spent that energy on self-care and being kind to myself. I strongly suggest that you don't become so critical of yourself. Make every attempt not to judge yourself as if you caused the miscarriage to happen. Nothing is wrong with you as a woman; it is said that within 2-4 weeks after a miscarriage, a woman ovulates again, so your chances of conceiving are excellent. Relax, God has you and the child He desires to enter the world through you in perfect timing. You two will not miss the opportunity to love each other endlessly.

When Faced With The News Of A Miscarriage

God is able to provide peace for you to find hope and joy. I've had one miscarriage – here's what I wished people knew about supporting women facing this experience. Miscarriage is incredibly common. According to the Mayo Clinic about one in five pregnancies end in miscarriage, but that number is likely higher as many early miscarriages go unreported. Be patient with the person who has had a miscarriage and reassure her that she is still a mother and nothing can change that. For the special woman that has lost a child through miscarriage. There is no right way to grieve, there is only your way, the way that is best for you.

One in five couples will experience a miscarriage in their journey to start a family. While miscarriages are common, many people who experience pregnancy loss find it difficult to process their loss as well as open up to family and friends. If someone you love has experienced a pregnancy loss or miscarriage, it can be hard to think of the right things to say.

You can help by praying for the grieving parent(s), send personal notes of encouragement, make yourself available to listen, ask dad and other siblings if they would like to talk. While it's true that a miscarriage hits mom the hardest, dad and the other siblings may be struggling with their own feelings of shock, confusion, and loss.

There are ways you can let dad and the other siblings know they're not forgotten by using question ended questions such as. "How are you doing?" or "Do you want to talk?" A phone call, a note, an invitation to have coffee or get ice cream will convey the message to the dad and other siblings "I know you've experienced a loss, too – and I care!"

The Grieving Process Involves Three Steps

1. Shock/denial
2. Anger/guilt/
3. Acceptance

Response:

You shall be mindful of how long you grieve taking as long as necessary not allowing anyone to rush your grieving period. I believe God in time will restore you. (Psalms 30:5)

Declaration:

I am a mother!

Day 12

Hello World It's Me _____ .

O' Tamar – Overcoming Molestation

This is my first time sharing my story of being molested as a child by a family member. I can honestly state I am whole (all inclusive), nothing missing and absolutely nothing broken. How do I know? I can tell my story without triggering any unresolved emotions towards my perpetrator. I will not use the name of my perpetrator to protect him. They honestly do not deserve to be judged by anyone for what they did. I honestly believe there could be psychological issues within their mind which led to the sexual abuse. I am in no way justifying neither excusing the abuse. I am rather empathic to my perceived thought of a mental condition which led him to believe what was done was somehow acceptable.

Why Now

For a long time, I keep my story silent, due to the false perception that good Christian families should never let anyone find out that they aren't completely thrilled with their lives. We should never complain to secular authorities (or anyone, for that matter, but especially secular authorities) about anything. It makes us bad witnesses.

It makes us bad Christians. And we might also be selfishly risking the destruction of our families because CPS will come and take us away. And there isn't anything better, right? After CPS destroys our families, we'll still be disciplined so destroying our families and our parents' good names would be for nothing, you might think.

Minority Families Do Not Teach Their Children About Sex

I believe me, like most minority girls, would get sex education lessons in public school. At a young age, I learn that there are things adults aren't allowed to do to us. I also learn that I have the right to say 'no.' I learn that if something is wrong, we should tell our teacher or call the police or inform another person of authority immediately. As a child it was required that each student female and male attended sex educational classes and learned what sex is. I admit I was clueless. It was like learning a foreign language after speaking in my language of birth all of my life. Learning a foreign language helps you to connect with the culture, while learning about sex education connects you with your growth and developmental stages in life.

A Christian Home

Growing up in a Christian family, we had to obey all adults unconditionally and instantly. I was taught that good Christian children who don't want to burn in hell submit to their parents. They submit to discipline from their parents, other adults, or older siblings. They submit to spankings. They do not talk back, and so on. If you are wrongly accused, you should still accept your punishment because you are a worthless sinful being and the punishment is probably good for you anyway. If you don't accept punishment when you're wrongly accused, that's a sin, so you need to be punished for that now. Catch 22. But, I was never taught about sex and being touched or inappropriately behavior signs to look for such as sexual suggestions or showing of genitals and the perpetrator calling it (my little secret friend).

Naughty Behavior

I was very young when my mother enlisted in the United States Military. So, my sister and I resided with my grandmother. It was during that time sexual abuse began at the age of three ending at the age of ten years. My mother's relocating to another state, was my salvation. Thank God! Seven years, I was touched inappropriately, force to grope genitals, at times endured forced penetration. However due to an overcrowded house, penetration was less frequent. Although the penetration was not as frequent the fondling was almost daily. Most occurrences occurred during the evening after supper, while my grandmother showered.

No matter where I sat my relative would sit next to me with a blanket touching me inappropriately. From couch to chair I moved; they would follow me. I remove their hand from my vagina, each time it was placed back in the same area. While simultaneously taking my hand placing it upon their genitals. This left me nauseated each time. This explains the reason why, I rarely smiled as a child not even on pictures. As a child

I did not comprehend despair but if it had a look, I wore it and sadness well. It was many years later, that I revealed to both parents the incidents of sexual abuse. I recall my mother; the classiest woman on earth asking, "why didn't you tell me?" I was so afraid and instructed as most victims are, not to say anything; to this day, my hero - dad has never asked me who. I ask why? He replied, "its best that I don't know." I discerned at that moment his desire to defend me was getting the best of him.

What To Look For

There are many signs of molestation that go unnoticed by parents or loved ones, but all are not easily noticed because the perpetrator often takes steps to hide their actions.

Some signs are easier to spot than others. Listen to your instincts. According to RAINN (Rape, Abuse & Incest National Network) here are a few signs to watch for:

- STD's or STI's (A sexually transmitted infection (STI) is a bacterial or viral infection passed from one person to another through vaginal, anal, or oral contact.
- Not wanting to be left alone with certain people or being afraid to be away from primary caregivers, especially if this is a new behavior.
- Sexual behavior that is inappropriate for a child.
- Bedwetting (especially if they are beyond the age)
- Excessively talking about sexual acts.
- Nightmares or fear of being left alone at night.

- Tries to avoid removing clothing to change or bathe
- Keeping children safe can be challenging since many perpetrators who sexually abuse children are in positions of trust—93 percent of child sexual assault victims know the perpetrator.
- Keeping a child away from the perpetrator may mean major changes in your own life, even if you are outside of the child's family.

Some indication that an adult is molesting a child are:

- Being very friendly with the child instead of being the adult.
- Giving the child a gift with no reason.
- Does not seem to have peers their own age.
- Very talkative to children about their own personal relationship (to build trust).
- Makes up excuses to be alone with the child.
- Express an excessive amount of interest in the child' sexual development.

Taking massive action isn't easy, but it is vital, it is not always easy to identify child sexual abuse.

Response:

Keep the lines of communication open with your child(ren).

Declaration:

From this day forward, I will no longer hold myself nor a perpetrator hostage. I free my mind, spirit, will, and emotions from the trauma of the past. (Luke 7:47)

If you are someone you know is a victim to sexual abuse. Seek help immediately, the National Sexual Assault Hotline (800. 656.HOPE and online.rainn.org) has helped more than 2 million people affected by sexual violence.

Day 13

Hello World It's Me _____.

A Sound Mind

The statement goes that a mind is a terrible thing to waste. Ignorance is not bliss. The Washington.edu; reports a misquoted statement, from The Energies of Men pg. 12 by Albert Einstein. The article stated that humans only use 10% of their brain.

There is no scientific evidence to support such claim. Perhaps when the 10% statement is used, it is meant that one out of every ten nerves cells are essential or used at one time. However, the statement was discovered; it bears a half truth, it is the mind of Christ that is a terrible thing to waste. God has entrusted each of us with his mind. He could have given his mind to any living creature. David said in (Psalms 8:4) "what is man that thou art mindful of him?" I believe God decided to house his intelligence in you and I. Why did God choose to house His creativity, ingenuity, resources, and wealth inside of man? Because man is the only created being that God made in his own image. There isn't any one word in the English language that could ever accurately express who God is. Language is the limitation of the mind. Do not expect the unlimited to leap forth into full expression through the limited. We must drop the complex and find simplicity before we can know God. We must become as a child. (Matthew 19: 14)

In Order To Understand This

A recalibration of the mind must take place in the event of you knowing the will and purpose of the world whence we came. The unspiritual self, just as it is by nature, can't receive the gifts of God's Spirit. There is no capacity for them. The Spirit can be known only by spirit - God's spirit and our spirits in open communion. Spiritually, we have access to everything God's Spirit is doing, and can't be judged by unspiritual critics. (1 Corinthians 14-16) asks a question "is there anyone around who knows the mind of God anyone who knows what He is doing?" This question has been long answered: Christ knows, and we have Christ's spirit.

What Is The Mind

The mind is medically described as /ˈmind/ a set of cognitive faculties that enables consciousness, perception, thinking, judgement, and memory - a characteristic of humans, but which also may apply to other life forms. The mind is best described as the seat of the soul. Soul-as referenced in (3 John 1:2) is compartmentalized in three components.

- The Mind: The intellect, gives you cognitive ability. The mind is the Heart which is the spiritual DNA of man.

- The Will: The ability to deliberately choose a healthy course of actions.

  When a person says they do not have to obey the Divine will of God, they are making a conscious choice to choose a course of life (another way) outside of the way of the Kingdom of God. Choosing another way of life, one cannot operate in the kingdom.

- The Emotions: the strong feelings that arise such as love, anger, guilt, joy, sadness due to circumstances.

Lastly, God hid his intelligence inside of you and I. Thus, a healthy mind is not an option. It is a must, for every human being! (Philippians 2: 5)

Response:

I will cast my net (awareness,) to the other side. Cast away wrong thoughts, wrong emotion which creates wrong living. Throw them over board forever!

Declaration:

My mind is healthy, fortified and resolute. I decree I shall not entertain wrong thoughts which release wrong emotions which produces false things that are not actually there.

Day 14

Hello world It's Me_____.

Love and Marriage Then Divorce

In 1997, I married my ex-husband who I thought I would remain married to until death. But it wasn't long after being married that my thoughts changed about us. Our first year of marriage was very hard. We became pregnant that first year and shortly thereafter while residing in the projects. Almost immediately I noticed mental instability and irrational behavior patterns. Yes, the same red flags I saw from the beginning, resurfaced. It is a true statement "the red flags you ignore in the beginning, will be the same red flags that end it."

That First Year Of Our Marriage

The first year My ex-husband, resentment grew more towards me. It showed the day he shelved me out of a moving vehicle while pregnant with our first daughter. Within the same year my ex-husband committed the first infidelity to add to that he stated he "didn't love me he loved his children from his previous marriage more." My ex-husband and I verbally fought savagely the first eight years of our marriage. We were angry and had dramatically opposing views on mostly everything. With intensity I would bite into him and he would bite into me. Almost like animals going after a bone with meat after not eating for a while.

Then there were times the sun would peek from behind the clouds, we'd laugh, and even spent quality time together. Those were the days I'd get the strength to try working on the marriage again for my children's wellbeing.

Exercise:

Three Ways To Better Communicate With Your Spouse.

1. Listen with the purpose to understand instead of with the intent to respond. Both spouses must be able to hear each other's concerns without getting defensive.
2. You and your spouse will learn to identify and express your needs and wants for one another as well as how to truly forgive.
3. Use more 'I' statements than 'U' statements. This decreases the chances of your spouse feeling like they need to defend themselves. For example, "I wish you would acknowledge more often how much work at home to take care of you and the children."

It is my fundamental belief that you will personally grow as your relationship grows.

Taking Care Of Business

My ex-husband and I owned several six-figure businesses; a Christian's Children's Learning Center, a Janitorial company and Construction Company. I spear headed a program through the state to help ex – offenders acquire employment through our construction company. Our construction company provided training in masonry and carpentry – my ex-husband, a skilled carpenter, trained ex-offenders in a classroom setting and in the field on property we acquired through state bids.

We stopped operations on all but one of those businesses when my ex-husbands' employer informed him of a need to relocate us to another state. The timing was perfect clients had slowed down to almost zero some months.

Prior to leaving from my home state; I received a prophetic word from the President of a bank in Tennessee. He stated, "God was going to prove to me that he loved me when my family and I arrived in our new destination." June 1, 2006 my family and I arrived. God did just what the Bank President said. We were blessed with a beautiful two-story home. My ex-husband's employer created a position for him. Things were going great. Finally, I was able to exhale at least for that moment. No sooner after being there, my ex-husbands instability and behavior changed for what seemed to be the worst.

I Do Not Love You

That year, my ex-husband registered for school, during that same time he met a new "friend" and started a study group; studying with her, he became more isolated from me. It reaffirmed the statement he made to me on our first year of marriage "I do not love you". On the surface, I was ok, but subconsciously the thought of not being loved by my husband haunted me. I wanted genuine love from him and couldn't quite understand why it was so hard for him to love me. It's not uncommon for an emotionally abused woman to ask herself many questions. Am I doing something wrong? Am I not pretty enough?

Exercise:

I want you to adhere to this thought, because you don't have a real answer as to why he or she committed infidelity, all you can do is blame yourself.

"If only I had complimented him more," you think.

"If only I had been more reasonable."

"If only I was prettier…thinner…funnier."

Can I tell you a secret? Every time you say, "If only…," you are cheating on yourself, and when you cheat on yourself, it's the ultimate betrayal. It means you don't value who you are. You don't respect your boundaries. You think you're aren't good enough. You believe you aren't pretty enough. If YOU feel that way about yourself, why is he or she not allowed to think the same? Why does he get all the blame and you take none of it?

Of course, the cheater is initially responsible. But once it's done and you find out, how you react to it is entirely up to you. If you can't raise your head high and know that what he or she did does not have anything to do with you, then you are cheating on yourself. I refer to it as self-sabotage, which is the highest form of sabotage known to mankind.

Exercise:

Three "S" On How To Love Your Spouse After Infidelity

1. Self - Esteem - we have to love ourselves before we can love anyone else. An affair can be detrimental to your self-esteem and gaining it back is very important.
2. Surrender – after you have built, your inner self and regain your strength surrender the idea and thought to get revenge. Revenge is a sign of weakness and a disoriented view of self. Revenge keeps you from focusing on transforming your life.
3. Start Over - you have to be excited about your new start and the road which lies ahead for the both of you. There will be obstacles, but look forward to sharing those obstacles with your husband or wife. It is good to be happy that you both are getting a second chance at love.

Someone Else's Misery

Uncontrollable thoughts of "being unloved" swamp in my head like a dolphin at sea, only at certain times I would come up for air. It is said you can die from someone else's misery – emotional states are as infectious as disease. You can feel you are helping the drowning man but you are only precipitating your own disaster. The unfortunate sometimes draw misfortune on themselves; they will also draw it on you if allowed. I found myself drowning in my ex-husband's misery. The emotional roller coaster was sickening, up one day, down the next day. I wanted off the roller coaster; I wanted the life I had imagine, you know, the big house, white picket fence, two children and a puppy. You know? The,

American dream. But that was not my reality and it was spiritually tearing at my soul. I wanted to change my reality. But How? The thought to remove the thorn from my side so I could heal was constant.

As a two- year old having temper tantrums, who wants his/her desire Now! Kicking, screaming, regardless of what their parents advises, until finally the parents gives in. I wanted out! No, matter how much I cried, yelled, waved my hands in the air asking God "why?" I had to face reality, my situation was a result of what I was saying, even more of what I thought of myself. Until I changed what I thought of myself, nothing in my reality changed. The power of what you say is insignificant when compared to the power of what you think.

Exercise:

Five Things To Reflect Upon

1. Am I ready to be a wife?
2. What is my emotional state?
3. What does a husband and a wife mean?
4. How is the relationship with your mother?
5. What example of a healthy wife have you studied?

PTSD

In 2007, my ex-husband was diagnosed with PTSD (Post Traumatic Stress Syndrome), an emotional condition with symptoms of numbness, fear, lack of trust, lower than normal self-worth, dissociation (not aware of the present moment) to name a few. My ex-husband was given a prescription medication and soon thereafter our marriage, spiraled downward to a sunken place. By the time the second infidelity transpired I was mentally drained and emotionally depleted. I'd had enough. This was my breaking point. The second infidelity was the final straw.

If you are someone else are showing symptoms of PTSD, please visit your nearest Veteran Administration office or visit the Veteran Affairs website at (www.va.gov).

The Separation

My ex-husband and I separated. I was left with no money, water, lights or food. I was in desperate need of a miracle. Who would have ever thought this would happen to me? I sure did not see this coming. I scrambled up the little money I could find, before asking family members for help. I had to get on welfare using food stamps to purchase food while I and my two children survived on two hundred dollars a month. Talk about beyond poverty, this was rock bottom. I tell you, the rock had jagged edges.

I couldn't get my head above water. Everywhere I turned for help, the answer would be 'no' or not at this time. Some days I felt I was losing my mind. I remember hearing a preacher say." "The waiting process between your confession and promise is the most difficult. He was correct! As the days became longer and nights shorter. I became angrier, waiting for the judge to finalize the divorce certificate. I wanted this eleven -year lie to be over.

If you've never walked this 'Green Mile', you might not be able to relate to the emotional and physiological shock that shoots through your mind like electrical volts. Emotionally the pain was intense. But I knew I could not succumb to defeat. I am a survivor!

The Dissolution Of The Marriage

It takes two willing people for the success of a marriage. After many years of feeling alone, isolated, and unloved, I stopped trying to hold on to someone that was obviously pulling away from me. I was not his problem, and I did nothing wrong. It is true, I was an excellent wife. After eleven years of marriage, I filed for a divorce. It was finally going to be over! Filing for divorce was half the battle.

Fighting the thoughts of being married never leave. Ignoring these thoughts is the best revenge. By acknowledging the memories, you give it existence and credibility. It is sometimes best to leave things alone. Do not be one of those people who look like paragons of patience but you're just afraid to bring things to a close. Leave the past in the pass.

Exercise:

How To Move On After Divorce

As hard as it is to look forward with hope during divorce, doing so will help you cope with the stress of divorce. Below are ten tips that will help you feel encouraged instead of discouraged.

1. Release the tears. Go ahead cry. No one marries with the idea that this is going to end someday.
2. Rediscover who you used to be and what you like.

3. Don't become paralyze focusing on what you do not have and what you have lost. Rather focus on what you do have and what you can do.
4. Make yourself a big deal. Work on understanding yourself and increasing your emotional value before enter into another relationship.
5. Find spiritual things to feed your soul and that speak to your mind.
6. Focusing on transforming your life from the inside out.
7. You will learn to sleep alone but also to come and go as you please on your own schedule.
8. Exercise and stay healthy! Exercise raises serotonin in your brain and helps fight depression.
9. Stay active in your community. Join a social club to establish professional and business relationships.
10. Remember you are not alone. There are other people who are now living your lifestyle and are there for you.

Now that you know that there is life after divorce. Let's discuss the process to receiving greater.

Process For Greater

Everyone who walks with God experiences the same kind of process. While there have been seasons in my life filled with apparent victory over major sin, little suffering, and seemingly unhindered communion with God. There have also been seasons filled with defeat, loss, affliction, and silence. In those moments, I feel tempted to "quit." But I'm reminded from God's word that this is all part of a process; namely, the process of sanctification. Having redeemed me from the grave, God is now transforming me and changing me into His image.

Are Being Transformed Into His Image With Ever-Increasing Glory (2 Corinthians 3:18b)

Trust God

Tough seasons of striping away, cutting through and tearing down, lead to the inner conversations of your heart with God about the purpose of this loss. There is a lesson of trust I am sure you needed to learn. Trusting God and His process is key to our faith journey, and yet for most of us, our experiences in our past can leave us scared to move forward or unsure of how to trust. This journal will walk you through a trust journey, however, you must first understand WHY it's important.

(Proverbs 3:5-10) is an exploration of that why. The first step in our "why" journey is to acknowledge our God and His plans. An understanding of the power, depth, and perfection of His plan must be acknowledged by you and me. When we embrace God's plan, and accept that His process is the best possible journey to be on, something happens. God MAKES our path straight and supernaturally removes the unnecessary apparatuses from our journey.

God Is At Work

In the moment where you are questioning whether or not God is working all things together for your good; you can trust the process of sanctification because God, tells us in (1Corithians 5:17). "Therefore, if anyone is in Christ, he is a new creation the old has passed away; behold, the new has come". It is the desire of God to bring the new. There is a direct correlation between acknowledging Him and the direction of our lives. I know it can be hard to trust the invisible and unforeseen, but you must extend your trust to God. When you don't that implies you are taking your future out of the hands of the Almighty and placing it into a dangerous place...the world.

Co-Laboring With God

There must be a cooperation with God. Any persons attempt to avert processing will endure underdevelopment and will never accomplish anything great. I learned a few years ago your gift may take you to the top, but your character is what keeps you on there. It was then that I embraced the statement *"I trust in your process."* God's process, if cooperated with, can be a quick and fruitful season.

I know you don't understand the situation you are facing. Because you don't understand or don't know what will happen, trust is necessary. It's not something you have to decide to do once. Don't hesitated. You must continually remind yourself that God has a plan regarding the 'unknown' situations in your life. He is in control, and He has your best interest at heart, all you have to do is trust.

It is a scientific fact all elements must endure a form of processing. Grapes must be crushed to make wine. Diamonds form under pressure. Olives are pressed to release oil. Seeds grow in darkness. You see, in life nothing is exempt from processing stage. The key resisted by many is endurance. We must endure. We tend to think only in terms of our endurance, but it is God's patient long-suffering which provides us with our chances to improve, affording us urgently needed developmental space or time. (2 Timothy 2: 3-5)

We cannot change the cards we are dealt just how the hand is played out to the end. At this moment if you feel crushed, pressured, pressed, and darkness, know that you are in the best season of your life for transformation/transmutation.

Stop Praying

At times, we pray to God. begging him to restore things He desires to move away from us. How insecure of us to not trust He knows what's best for us. For eleven years, my ex-husband and my children had become the center of my world. Surely, I thought life would have given me back the joys I attempted to create for my family. However, life is under no obligation to give what we expect.

Was it healthy to be consumed with my family need's? Is this God's idea for marriage? That the wife neglects herself, to do the patchwork for the tapestry of her family? I am aware there are several answers to these questions? However, I expected God to restore what I and many others considered an unhealthy family dynamic. These are the things we do when we don't understand the purposes of God.

When we lack understanding we will pray for God to restore things that will satisfy our temporal needs. Fortunate for me, restoring that marriage was not the blueprint of God. His restoration plan for me, was removing the very things I held precious and dear.

God Had Another Plan

One morning while my daughter, my son and I were praying for my ex – husband, my daughter said "mom stop this, we can't keep doing this, my dad has made his decision. You must move on!" "Mom, look at you, you are *beautiful,* and some other man is going to love you the way you need to be loved." Out of the mouth of my own child, wisdom came. That day, I received what my daughter stated, but it was not an easy process to do. I struggled. Realizing that my ex-husband was no-longer there was a tough pill to swallow. In the back of my mind, I had hoped he would 'come to his senses' and reclaim his abandoned family.

 Let's take a look at this: I prayed he still left. I prayed some more, and we got divorced. Do you see the pattern, it is not that prayer does not work, it just works only according to the will of God concerning you and I. My ex-husband returning was not my immediate problem. God spoke to me *"Angela, you do know that the king's heart is in my hands, and I can turn it whatsoever way I choose? "Just as I have the king's heart, I could have turned your ex-husbands heart back towards you a long time ago."* (Proverbs 21:1) Wow!

There was an even greater spiritual concern of the Father for me. A spirit of feeling abandonment was my real problem. I had rejection and abandonment issues, long before my ex-husband came into the equation. His leaving was the catalysts for me to deal with the issues of my soul. A soul that is bleeding will bleed on everyone it comes in contact with if it is not healed. I had bleed on my husband for years.

Yes, a good home maker, but emotionally detached from him. I never healed from the first infidelity on top of the childhood trauma I endured. I should not have married anyone, until I was emotionally whole. I can only imagine the emotional abandonment he felt I caused him as well. I needed my soul saved, healed from deep rooted issues. His leaving opened my eyes to see. He was no longer my focus. I was my on-stumbling block and it was from that moment transformation began. I started from childhood writing down every name of every person who had wrong me, until I had forgiven each one. This was my new birth into a higher life, into spiritual consciousness of who I am in God, the power to heal and overcome.

If you are going through a divorce. It is not the end of your life. However, it is the end of the life you share with your spouse. You will survive. Trust me, I did! I say to you what my daughter said to me, "Look at you, really look at you, you are beautiful."

Response:

Love will find you again, if you will allow it.

Declaration:

Today, I closed this chapter. A new chapter opened for me. I will miss the new things that are happening for me by whining long over what has happened towards me. This is not the end of my life; just the ending of an old thing and welcoming the new.

Session III

I AM Coming OUT

Day 15

Hello World It's Me _____.

Rejection Bounce

There is relevance in being rejected and not being normal. You cannot expect to be remembered if you follow and flow with the crowd. The crowd is where average and normal people are. When the crowd is walking in one direction those who are rejected by men are climbing a mountain in a different direction. I see women rising all over the world, who have the understanding, when it comes to purpose, it is never discovered looking for it in someone else. Women, would rather endure rejection, than be a cloud without reign.

Women of great magnitude suffer from rejection, more than our male counterpart. However, we are in an hour God's hand is resting upon women all over the world. I see it in the women in my life, who have climbed great mountain and are exceling, coming into view from obscurity. Women are rising like lioness', to change our world.

The lioness symbolizes a courageous, fearless hunter. There is a call for women to arise from fear to live bold, courageous walking fully into their God given purpose. For every woman reading this book. You possess power and dominion. You can and you shall prevail. What was designed to destroy you is the same thing God will use to promote you. Women all over the world are "rising" out of deep, dark places into the light to be seen as cutting-edge women who are on the leading edge of their field of influence.

Some Important Facts About Rejection.

1. Rejection is the act of refusing to accept, to use, to submit, make use of or believe in something or someone.
2. Rejection is one of the hardest things in life for any person to have to handle.
3. Rejection is an impaired ability to give and receive love.
4. Rejection is a process in which the immune system of a body attacks an organ or tissue either its own or transplanted. Sounds a lot like the Body of Christ.
5. Rejection victimizes its prey causing them to feel worthless and unwanted.
6. Rejection employs a spirit of self-pity as it right hand man to drive people away and allow abandonment and isolation to move in.
7. Rejection taunts with one failure after another in hopes you will say, "*I give up!*"

Don't give up! Do you have a spirit of rejection at work in your life? Everyone experiences rejection at some time but here are 10 protentional indicators of the spirit of rejection at work.

10 Fruits Of A Spirit Of Rejection At Work In Your Life.

1. You find yourself **comparing** your circumstance or situations with others, and you never seem to **measure** up.
2. You feel like you missed out on life's opportunities and now it's too late.
3. No amount of **encouragement** is enough to **convince** you of your **worth**.
4. You feel **rejected** if you are not **greeted** or acknowledge by those in **superior** position than you.
5. You constantly seek the **approval of others** and suffer from people please and attention seeking.
6. You are easily offended or embarrassed from discipline or correction.
7. You are always trying to **prove** yourself in **public**.
8. You reel like you are on the outside looking in during interactions with people.
9. You **think** you could do a **better** job than the current person or teach if you are given the opportunity.
10. You believe no one **understands** you, or what you are going through.

Hidden

Nowadays women are excelling in each and every field (science, fashion, education, officers, doctors, politicians etc.) You too are capable of excelling and achieving great success for yourself, your tomorrow and your world. You must see yourself through the lens of God and what He desires for you to do before you can do it. You must prepare yourself for what you want, day and night. In his book 360 Degree Leader, John

Maxwell states how you have to realize its' normal for any person to want recognition, and leaders are the same. The fact that leaders in the middle of the pack are often hidden – as a result they don't get the credit or recognition they desire and deserve. But if you consistently deliver the goods, you will be noticed."

Not everyone will appreciate or understand the assignment you have, and it's not intended for them to. But it's important that you understand your destiny clearly. A cute anecdote from Nobel Prize- winner Charles H. Townes Illustrates this well. Townes commented, it's like the beaver told the rabbit as they stared up at the immense wall of Hoover Dam, "No I didn't actually build it myself, But, it was based on an idea of mine. Every position has value.' In studying the lion, I discovered something so interesting and had the thought, that if more women would value this trait. What could we accomplish?

The lioness stays hidden as long as possible, slinking along on her belly when necessary, staying hidden in the grass (which is often the same color as her fur), in order to get as close to the prey as possible. When she (and her fellow lionesses) finally get noticed, and the jig is up, it's a mad sprint to the prey. What a skill to have to stay hidden for as long as possible, until the opportune time. Most, people struggle with this, because they are afraid of missing out on something. And they move pre-maturely. Missing the opportunity, which sometimes does not immediately cycle back. Be patient. You may be hidden at the moment. But soon the jig will be up and it will be your time of revealing.

Women are raising up all over the world who will defy the odds. Sir Walter Newton is reported to have acquired his marvelous knowledge of Mathematica's and physics with no conscious effort. Mozart said of his beautiful symphonies, they just came to him. Descartes had no ordinary regular education and to quote Dr. Hudson, there is a power which transcends human reasoning and is independent of manipulation. And that power lies in you and I.

You may feel like an ordinary woman, but you are an extra ordinary woman with a little dipping sauce. Because you know how to draw upon the mind of God, and exemplify the power of a sent one. Everything has been set by God to work for you.

Broken Members

We are in the age where people suffer from effects of rejection - we don't want people to dislike us. Truth is, not everyone will love and appreciate you. As a matter of fact, some people regret the day they met you. You must be okay with that.

Most people who reject you really reject themselves. (1 Corinthians 12:14) indicates, "that there are many members yet one body". We are all one body. Rejecting your brothers and sisters in Christ is like rejecting parts of your body. We can get plastic surgery to alter structure. But overtime those alterations will reveal who you aren't. Rejection is the greatest enemy of the spiritual life because it contradicts the sacred voice of the Father who calls us the beloved.

Being the beloved constitutes the core truth of your existence. You must not quiver at rejection. Rejection will be common among those who are successful. The names Opah Winfrey, Michael Jordan, Walt Disney and Steve Job, aren't usually associated with failure. But before these successful super stars made it big in their respective industries, they first failed, were fired, or heard the word "no" countless times. But they never gave up.

No matter how many times, those closest to you or society may reject the idea of you, you mustn't reject you neither - give up. Soon you will hear 'yes, it's time, we love your idea, we want you, you are hired.' You also mustn't settle for mediocrity.

Mediocrity always attacks excellence. Anyone who has an agreement with mediocrity will always attack you and feel uncomfortable in your presence. May you rise up reclaim your spiritual lineage and take your position in this world for it is time to say "Hello World It's Me – I AM here."

Exercise:

How To Heal From A Spirit Of Rejection.

Step 1. Identify the weakness of stronghold of rejection.

When the military wants to invade a city, they send someone to check the weakest point of the city first. They would identify the openings to invade, and learn what holds the city together so they would know the best place to begin the attack. The same thing works with identifying the weakness that allows rejection to enter, identifying the weakness also identifies what strongholds to pull down in the mind. Stronghold can not access your life without an opened door.

Step 2. Closing the Door.

Double-mindedness begins with rejection and opens the door for an unstable identity, personality disorder and anxiety. The close the door is by forgiving every person who has rejection you, one person at a time. Every time you forgive someone who has hurt, rejected or abandon you, you close a door. As you work your way through the list, you notice that you can breathe a little better. The air way isn't as obstructed as before. You can breathe in the outside world a little more clearly, with fewer doors to close on your path.

Step 3. Receiving.

One of the most common reactions people have to a rejection is to become *self-critical*. We list all our faults, lament all our shortcomings, and chastise ourselves endlessly. This happens when there is a misunderstanding our identity, one of the greatest travesties we face today, is not knowing who and what we are. The world is suffering from an identity crisis. It is vital that we base our identity, who we are, upon what God's Word says about us. When we do, we become virtually immune from the devastating and hurtful effects of rejection and abandonment. God promises never to leave or forsake us, so when our identity is based upon what He says of us, we can be assured that we're not going to face rejection coming from Him.

For God Has Said: I Will Never Leave You, And I Will Never Forsake You. (Hebrews 13:5)

Response:

Anything you reject you are already giving it too much of your attention. When beasty (thoughts) come to you, you will turn to your creator and remember His thoughts toward you. This is your time to leave your mark in earth. The moment of all moment that define or give meaning to your life.

Declaration:

I will no longer reject myself, abandonment has to go now! Say Aloud… Today I declare, I reject rejection!

Day 16

Hello Worlds it's Me _____.

I Am Every Woman

I celebrate what every great woman in the history of our time has achieved. Those times where success in certain fields, were looked at as being only for men. In our day, women are sensing the great need and are seizing the opportunities to be world class leaders. Women of all races all across the world are coming from obscurity. It is as if they simultaneously hear the sound "it's your time to be seen, your time to be noticed, and your time for others to observe you. You are one of those women….This 16th day was written especially for you.

There Is Nothing Ordinary About You

You are the original thought in the Divine Mind of God. You, hold the idealistic pieces that have long been missing in the woes of society. Women, it has been long that you should have awaken and coming into view. I see you, "rising" out of deep, dark places into the light of your being. It is love that awakes you, empowers you, and equips you to tackle the greatest wall, and climb the highest mountain. Just to come into view to save that one.

Many are waiting on you. You are the creative center, from which increase is given off to all. Your coming into view is vital. You thought you were waiting on something or someone special to happen before you, manifest yourself. The release you are waiting on is not determined by God or a celestial being. It is determined by you. The choice has always been given to you and it is yours. This is why it is said in (Ephesian 5:14) "Wake up, sleeper, rise from the dead, "AND" Christ will shine on you." God does not want to do for you; what He will do for you until you awaken.

When You Wake Up You Become The Power That Does the Work

You are to take an initiative in the fulfillment of your calling. Poet Edgar A. Guest wrote: "You can do as much as you think you can. But you'll never accomplish more; If you're afraid of yourself, young man. There's little for you in store. For failure comes from the inside first. It's there if we only knew it. And you can win, though you face the worst. If you feel that you're going to do it." You have the power ally your conscious self with that sleeping giant within you, rouse him daily to the task, and those "superhuman" deeds will become your ordinary, everyday accomplishments.

Every Woman Has An Open Future Not A Closed Future

Woman, you are not just a simple person with complexity. The power of the creator is in you; to create the reality you desire to see. You hold the trump card of your destiny. Nothing happens by chance. Every Action (including thought) has a reaction or consequence. The law of perpetual states that every person can change their conditions in life. You must engage in ACTION that supports it. The reality of what you think, speak or feel; you will become. When you desire to see a different reality, you make different choices. Now, there is the favor of God upon you, but your choices determine the outcome. Never stop to question whether you can do it. See only the urgent need. Concentrate all your thoughts, all your energy on that one thing—never doubting, never fearing—and God which is in all of us waiting only for such a call will answer your summons and give you the strength—not of one person but of, ten! It matters not whether you are a banker, educator, or a stay at home mom. Make what you are doing interesting to yourself and others will find it exciting also.

Response:

You, the advancing woman, hold to a clear mental image of yourself as successful women who obey the laws of faith, purpose, and gratitude. She will cure every curable case she undertakes, no matter what remedies she may use.

Declaration:

The image that I see of myself is clear. I no longer see myself through a blurred scope according to the two eyes on my head but through the lens of the Spirit of God.

Day 17

Hello World it's Me _____.

Free My Soul

Your personality is a set of characters that differentiate you from another. It is said that your soul is the seat of your personality. It is the driving force behind why you do the things you do momentarily or over an extended time. It's what sets your uniqueness apart. No two people are the same, similar yet not the same.

The Mind Is the Spiritual Womb for Conception

The soul and the spirit are connected but separable (Hebrews 4:12). The soul is the essence of humanity's being; it is what we are. In the beginning God created man and he breathed into that man and he became a living soul. Every human being live from their soul. Our soul keeps record of every incident that has happen to us in life. The spirit is the immaterial part of humanity that connects with God. Soul is the immaterial part of humanity that connects to our mind, will and emotions. According to Blue Letter Bible: soul in the Hebrew connotations is nnaphas...which also deals with the emotional aspect of the MIND, and the area of the mind that is sensitive to atmospheric movement or activity. In one translation, the term soul is where we get our word soookiii socio. It is where we get the psychological which means the mind and it is where we get behavioral patterns. This is also where each of us gets our emotional expression. Charles Fillmore, author of 'Teach us to Pray', wrote: "we make our soul out of the thoughts and words we entertain. Consequently, we should be very careful in choosing our words. Our words are the means by which we convey Spirit to character and its structure." With our words, we tend to give things power that otherwise have no power. Life and death are in the power of the tongue, and they that love it shall eat the fruit thereof. (Proverbs 18:21)

Every word is a spirit. Every word has its root in an idea. Whether this idea is reflected from within or not. Words, once released are planted into the atmosphere of our mind at the most opportune or inopportune time they shall manifest.

In The Beginning

In the beginning was the Word, and the Word was with God, and the Word was God' (John 1:1). We could all learn something from this well-known Bible verse. Looking beyond the religious connotation, there is a message to be found in this for everyone. According to the Law of Attraction, words consist of vibration and sound. It is these vibrations that create the very reality that surrounds us. Words are the creator; the creator of our universe, our lives, our reality. Without words, a thought can never become a reality. This is something that we have been taught throughout history, as far back as the Bible, which writes of 'God' – saying 'let there be light' and light was created. So, what do we learn from this"? If our words are thoughts, then surely, they are the most powerful tool that we have. We should use the most powerful words to manifest what we are desiring. Everything, begins with a word. We should only pick the very best words in order to create our very best reality.

Response:

Get quiet, pray, meditate on the Lord, who is your keeper. Your soul wants to 'master' you, however God will not suffer your foot to be moved.

He Will Not Let Your Foot Slip-- He Who Watches Over You Will Not Slumber. (Psalms 121:3)

Declaration:

I will separate myself from the thoughts of my soul and will never give anything a power that never had a power. My emotions are controlled by my spirit.

Day 18

Hello Worlds It's Me _____.

No One Else Looks Like Me

In the world of scientific discovery, there is nothing that is quite so important as the discovery of self. We are very much concerned about discovering new continents, new planets and North and South Poles. Rarely ever do we bestow a thought upon the greatest of all these discoveries, which is the discovery of that which constitutes the reality of man. (Psalms 139:14) says, "I praise you because I am fearfully and wonderfully made; your works are wonderful, I know that full well". (Psalms 139:13) reads, "For you created my innermost being; you knit me together in my mother's womb".

Spiritual Awarness

We are in the process of getting back our expanded spiritual awareness. God is awakening you to the new thing going on long ago within you. (Isiah 43:19) says, "Behold I do a new thing in you; do you not perceive it?" What seems like a season of pain may actually be the "new thing" God is doing. He will allow pressure to be applied to heighten the awareness of who you are. You're always told that you are human being, but we are also humans doing. We were not created a human being; we are created spirit beings bearing the fullness of the image and the knowledge of God before we came out of heaven and were made into a human image. We are spirits slowed down to visibility. The very life of God actually chooses to live inside of you and I. We will need to meditate upon that day and night, if not, we will never get a revelation of who we really are and what we have inside of us. It is about who we are. The (Omniscience, omnipresence, and omnipotence) of God actually lives inside of you and I. We are a host for a realm of government that God is choosing to become an expression through and of Him in the face of the earth.

Your Authentic Voice

Frances Bennett says "Never doubt your own authentic voice when you are speaking from an awakened, open-hearted awareness. "No matter how small or quiet that voice may be, it will be heard, not only by you but by others. It will resonate, as all authenticity always does. All authentic voices matter. A wonderful thing begins to happen and unfold naturally and almost effortlessly when they are heard. Your authentic voice always carries a powerful anointing of the Holy Spirit!"

When you come into the same frequency and shadow of Heaven, you will speak from the heart of God. You will speak the mind, will and purpose of Christ. His sound will be released through you into earth. No one sounds like you, you are an unrepeated miracle whose time has come!

Response:

You are not strange - there is nothing about you that needs to change other than your 'thinking' nothing about you physically need to change.

Declaration:

There is no power (physical, social or religion) nor external force that can have any power or dominance over me, unless I yield my members to its power.

Day 19

Hello Worlds It's Me_____.

Being Broke Is Not A Joke

I have been so broke until it was funny (no seriously). I've been financially broke, to the point, I couldn't find enough money to place gas in my car. There were days, I did not know what my children and I would eat. If there was a bottom to the pit, I had hit it and it clanged loudly. My friends, and I would often be each other salvation. I recalled a day one of my friends stated, *'if you make it to church'* I will give you gas money. Likewise, I'd return the favor. Somehow, we developed this buddy system, "when I had it, so did they". Externally you would not have known the financial struggle I was in. I believe, knowing how much I could bare, God kept me together so that I would not have to endure further shame.

I recall crying out to God *"hey God it's me-Angela, do you see me?"* I was in the sea of despair. On top of being broke, I was served a 7-day eviction notice. At this stage in my life, I could only imagine a different life other than the one I was experiencing. The more I imagined life differently, the more my circumstance began to change for my good. To imagine is to willfully picture the thoughts we have been thinking and putting ourselves in mental participation with it. The words that God had been showing me regarding my life, came into my spirit. I am aware, that this information was brought up into my conscious mind for me to imagine them until manifestation. I would think these spiritual thoughts and marry them with words until they came forth. I created mental pictures and I began to see the reality, the truth of what I was thinking about.

Here's an example: I saw myself relocating from Florida to Wisconsin I saw the car I would travel in. I saw the stops I would make along the way for gas and rest. I also saw the welcome to Wisconsin sign as I entered into the state mentally before physically crossing the state line. It was soon thereafter I along with my children moved to Wisconsin. Initially my left brain (analytical side) wrestled with the idea. However, the more I yielded to what the Holy Spirit was downloading from within, the more I imagined myself traveling. I stand firm in not doing anything unless I have first seen it in my mind. We must educate our mind to see what we see so that our mind (analytical side) does not reject the spiritual dimensions or miracle manifestations because they are too marvelous beyond HUE (man) mental capacity or our reasoning. We must increase the borders of our mind and break free from our mental limitations if we desire to manifest our reality. When our mind gets accustomed to such expansions soon our faith will flourish.

Example two: I am self-employed all my income comes from my business. One day I imagined this, notice I did not say 'I need' (when you hold on to thoughts of need you push things further away from you). I was imagining receiving money into my account. It was a struggle manifesting due to blockage in my soul of unforgiveness and guilt. Once I rid my soul of these, my eye and ear gate opened. The eye and ear gate are necessary elements for development of the mind. We learn to see and hear what God is saying. We are helping to coordinate the mind with the revelation flow that is coming into our spirit. You must see yourself doing it first. If we mock and laugh at it, in our mind, the reality of what we are imagining will be impossible to become fulfilled. After removing the blockage, I saw money that God wanted me to have. I receive it, to receive means to accept what was *always* mine. With my mind I acknowledged the gift that God was presenting to me cooperating and coordinating with the spirit and thus allowing the negative thought patterns to drown in the "red sea". I had to develop a habit of seeing the reality of the money already in my possession. This process took several months of 'action' to breakthrough. We cannot be in haste when operating in faith. We must allow patience to have her perfect work in and through us.

The creative law of action when engaging in actions that support your prophesy. You must 'ACT'. After which you have exhausted all measures, God of the universe will do what you cannot. Many are waiting on release, yet the release you are looking for is not determined by God, it is determined by you. A biblical reference in (Ephesians 5:14) says "wake up, sleeper, rise from the dead, and (consequentially) Christ will shine on you."

When God awakens you He also awakens things for you in heaven. It is the responsibility of every believer to take initiative in fulfilling our prophesy. When you wake up, you become the power that does the work. God has given you the power to correct the past, rectify the present and open the future. The law of perpetual states every person can change their conditions in life. You must engage in action that supports this change. You must "ACT", do something, get up, go forth and forge ahead. The power of the creator is in you, to create the reality you desire to see, and to manifest the prophesy. Nothing happens by chance. Every action (including thought) has a reaction or consequence. The reality you desire to see now, is in your favor. What do you desire to see?

Exercise:

- Replace negative thoughts with positive.
- Train your ear and eye gate to hear God.
- Develop habits to see the reality you desire.
- Do not laugh and mock at what comes into your spirit.
- Change your belief. Unbelief paints a picture that endorses fear.
- Change your mental thought vibrations if you desire to see a different world.

Response:

If you have received personal prophesy about traveling the country imagine yourself boarding a plane! If you have the poise to keep quiet when unbelief is talking, the day will come when Father God gives you the opportunity to travel.

Declaration:

I decree today, my eye and ear gates are developing my mind, so that I can learn and see what God is saying to my spirit. I decree today is my last day of being financially broke!

Day 20

Hello Worlds It's Me _____.

Caught in a Net

Author George Orwell states; reality exist in the human mind and nowhere else. If this is true, then we must exercise the thought of our mind. We must get our mind in shape by progressing forward. Just like weight lifting you first must break down the muscle to build. What does this mean? Getting my reality to align with my thoughts. I can attest at times it became a struggle. I was moving forward, I was proactive, but nothing was changing. I continued to see myself in the same cycle. Meeting the same people yet different faces. yet same people from a former season. It is said people that we meet are either reflections of a repeated cycle or guides towards a new start. Why was this happening? I believe my life was under mental arrest.

So, it had me to think of what I had done over the course of my life? I was thinking, changing, progressing and moving forward yet my circumstances, were not changing. Neither did I have the mental capacity or ability to progress forward.

Johnathan David, Author of Breakthrough Thinking: "states the sub-conscious retains every single experience from our past. It stores the type of feelings felt and expressed in each situation involved. It records the opinions, views, and conclusions we made in those situations. It also keeps the record of what our spirit felt and how it responded during these situations. Inspiration of faith, the excitement and joy released by our spiritual breakthroughs are all retained and recorded in the sub-conscious. The function of the sub-conscious is to open up memory files on our whole life, recording them specifically under different categories, in which the situations and experiences that are recorded may vary from person to person."

Because we live from our sub-conscious mind, it has a capability to be under arrest. In other words, sub-consciously there is a forceable pressure that prevents forward progression. I identify this as being *caught in a net*. The forceable pressure in the atmosphere of my mind in the form of negative debunking thoughts. My thoughts were warring against the members of my mind. Although making faith declarations I was stuck!

As I further investigated, I had to examine my soul. We are spirit beings, but we live from our soul which encompass'- the mind, will and emotions. I discovered sub-consciously situations that occurred, created a deep impact on me. Whether negative or positive, each occurrence has been registered in all its fullness in my subconscious. My past was now superimposing upon my present. I came to the realization that two things were causing me to be stuck were *unforgiveness and guilt*. These 'twins' were poisoning my mind and kept me locked in my circumstances. Unforgiveness and guilt have been programmed into the subconscious mind. Those who are television watchers can attest to hearing talks about unforgiveness and guilt. Television is comprised of programs that make you angry by airing all the negative things that are happening in the world to invoke anger and to reprogram your mindset. All negative things can be erased from our mindset. It is a process I call to debunk a system and replacing it with an even greater force. There are steps to take to become and remain unstuck. How do we do this?

First, we must break the falsehood that the opposite of love is hate. The opposite of love is guilt, guilts comes after a traumatic situation such as a broken heart and it brings along condemnation with it. According to Webster Dictionary, condemnation is the action of condemning someone including yourself to a punishment or to a sentence. Anytime you harbor guilt in your heart or mind, you are punishing and sentencing yourself and wishing upon yourself the same thing you are wishing upon someone else. You are sentencing yourself into a mental prison over and over again until you become ashamed. Whenever you feel ashamed you repeat that same action in your mind as if it just happened. This is why I have written this book.

Women we need to heal in order to manifest and experience the breakthroughs that God has for us. We must heal! We must get unstuck from the mental time warp of repeating and living out the same cycle year after year. In order to do this, we must change our thought patterns. The same thinking pattern will keep you in the same rhythm as the former season. Secondly getting unstuck requires a soul detoxification. We must cleanse out, rid ourselves of the things that do not belong. Things that have been stuck in our mind for years, causing us to remain in a time warp (cycle) are the same things that reshaped our mental construct year after year.

Here Are Three Areas To Examine When Getting Unstuck

- Eyes - The windows to the soul.
- Hands – When we lay hands we release the spirit of God.
- Heart – Spring forth the issues of your life.

Think about something that has cause you guilt, on a scale of one to ten, I want you to rate that experience. Next, I want you to imagine laying your hands upon the thing that hurt you. Lastly, release it from your heart. Say out loud I forgive you and I forgive myself for the mental prison I have held myself captive in for years. I can't undo the past, but I can choose to find peace. Forgiving myself or others is a way to let go and move on.

Exercise

- Believe in yourself.
- Discover your purpose.
- Change your perspective.
- Start with the small things.

You may need to change your life purpose if it no longer inspires you. Or if you feel you haven't had a purpose, this is a great time to define one. Asking yourself the following questions will assist you in considering your life purpose.

- What am I good at?
- Who inspires me the most and why?
- What are my favorite things to do now?
- What makes me feel good about myself?
- What were my favorite things to do in the past?
- When do I enjoy myself so much or become so committed to something that I lose track of time?

Response:

You will not allow certain people to come into your life with the same characteristic of the personality of someone from the past. You will not relive the situations as though it happened.

Declaration:

There are some serious changes about to take place in my mind and in my life.

Day 21

Hello World It's Me _____.

Finding My Home - Less

Many days I questioned the day of my existence, God "why am I here, what is my purpose". I am sure we all have at one time or another ask similar questions. It seemed struggles, heartaches and pain became my sentence in life. As a child some things I brought on myself, being stubborn and rebellious. However, most I didn't, people had done me wrong, for no reason. I had endured so much at a very early age. I fought many days, not to become bitter, angry, and resentful at God for releasing me into the earth during this era. Most days I felt out of place. I never belonged. Psychologically, I was opposite of everyone close to me. I guess I was wired differently. But why me? Why was I rejected and abandon by those I loved?

Was This God's Way of Tempting Me

I know it is said God doesn't tempt anyone. However, in (Genesis 22:1) God, tempted Abraham. Not as it regards to Abraham sinning against God. The word tempt in this scripture means to **evolve**, to **assay** and **adventure**. God desires for what is placed within each of us, to evolve. God does not want us to be satisfied with the status quo and wants us to continue to raise to a higher consciousness (spiritual awarness and spiritual perception). The only way to rise to higher consciousness is to think through the mind of God or as Jesus instructed Peter in (John 21:6) cast your nets to the right side; means to involve yourself in purposeful meditation. Purposeful mediation is to turn our sight from the external to the internal. Seeing in the spirit the things God downloads. So how did I begin my quest for answers? I began by getting spiritual illumination of the Kingdom that is within me.

For, Behold, The Kingdom Of God Is Within You. (Luke 17:21

Perhaps you are wondering, what was I looking for? I was looking for my home not just your typical spot. What I was in search for was much deeper a much richer place than life itself. Far grander than what this physical world could ever offer me. Although physically I was homeless. The home I was on a quest for was not physical, it was my spiritual place. The spiritual void was greater than my need for a physical residence. I was homeless spiritually; without a spiritual domain. I was living from my e-motions (energy in motion), you know the feeling you get after things happened or did not happened as you'd hoped, depression, joy, sorrow, high's, lows. I had a vagabond mentally. My mind would wonder seamlessly like water down the river bank.

All Alone

Most days, I felt cut off from society, and alone. Feeling alone can happen anywhere. It is not the same as physically being alone. Each of us are capable of spending time alone with ourselves and not feel lonely. By contrast, sometimes we can be in a crowd of people and still feel alone. The feeling of loneliness comes from inside ourselves, our thoughts, and our emotions. It is not an external factor. And because it exist within, we can't seek external solutions.

Many life situations can lead one to feel alone. Periods of life changes are times when many people are especially prone to feeling alone. For instance, when you move to a new place, start a new job, or end a relationship. In these situations, you lose support systems you previously had in place and may find yourself looking for new people to spend time with and depend upon. Remember, the feeling of being alone isn't external. Seeking someone to fulfill the void, will undoubtingly leave you with people who are as empty barrels making a loud noise.

Questions Anyone

I, was on a quest. A journey to discover what was this thing happening within me. I initiated this adventure asking myself questions. To, ask QUEST-IONS is to be on a quest to generate (ions) whether, positive or negative electrical charges from within. To ask QUEST-IONS you're 'seeking' or on a quest to discover answers. Man-made answers will only put you on a quest to serve in their dimensional reality. Have you ever wondered why Adam was called Adam? In ancient times a name such as Adam didn't really exist. The name served as symmetry or was symbolic to the word Atoms. Atoms are known as a collection of (ions). If you were to dissect the name Adam, it would look like this; (A) Dam in

Hebrew means "Blood" The Blood consist of "ions" or a collection of ATOMS/ADAMS. The story of Jesus who is considered the last Adam, dying on the cross depicts to us what the blood expresses. The blood, expresses a spiritual principle that has been introduced into the mind of mankind through the purified Jesus. The blood of Jesus can be appropriated and used to the purification of the mind and the healing of the body. Through His experience on the Cross, where His precious blood was spilled, through His suffering there, Jesus lowered His consciousness to the consciousness of mankind. Thereby, administering to the whole (hue) man race a blood transfusion, imparting to man the properties of being that will restore him to his divine estate.

Such a transfusion not only revives us in temporal illness but begins in the body a purifying and energizing process that will finally save us from death and gives us abundant life. The life contained in God's Word is spiritual energy that purifies and redeems from sin and death.

The Redeemed Of The LORD; And You Will Be called, Sought Out, A City Not Forsaken. (Isaiah 62:12)

At This Juncture You Are Probably Wondering What Does Any Of This Have To Do with Being Home-Less?

This is where you begin your quest, by seeking or turning within so that all the answers to your questions are discovered. I like to refer to this as your spiritual treasure hunt. Before we begin our quest, it is vital that we understand this principle found in (Luke 17:21) "Neither shall they say,

Lo here! or, lo there! for, behold, the kingdom of God is within you."

The answers we are all in search for are not outside of you and I. God did not put your answers in another man. Man can only give you their ideology which enslaves you to a system, which controls the mind. The answers are and have always been within you. This thought, put me in remembrance of the revelation of the 'seed' of greatness that is inside each of us.

Everything including idea's begins in seed form. All living things, you and I, to every tree in the forest began as a seed and small in size. God knows what inside of every seed planted in earth and declares what's inside of each seed to manifest.

"But we have this treasure in earthen vessels, that the excellency of the **power** may be of God, and not of us." (2 Corinthians 4:7)

The power to produce an idea is the same power to a higher degree to manifest that idea in material form. How is this possible? It is because the "seed of greatness" within you is the divine mind of God. The divine mind of God is the resistless power, it is the force of God with which we can perform otherwise seemingly impossible undertakings. In order for you to walk in this power and anointing you must come into the knowledge of your position in the capacity of your purpose "Ye are gods" are all of you are children of the most High (Psalms 82:6). We are earthy representatives of God in flesh. It is the responsibility of every believe to represent – God. This includes His ideology, His creativity, His mind, all of that which makes up the essence of God to the world.

We can only do this if we know who we are. Who are we? Ask yourself the question. Contrary to the consensus thought of the general populace we are not our hands, our feet, our eyes. We are not even our names these are anatomical parts and titles that we possess. What then is this reality we wake up to every morning 365 days a year, 24 hours a day 7 days a week? I'm glad you asked. Our human constitution vibes with every definitive of gods.

We are tri-part deity of Spirit, Soul, and Body (human nature by rite of passage via the feminine energy vortex the birth canal) thus we are god consciousness having a human experience. We are living souls-the soul is a composite of generated electromagnetic current (the breath of God) and can never be destroyed because our spirit is eternal, always has been, always will be.

The soul cannot die however it can be neglected while existing on earth and become dormant. It is to be noted anything that is dormant is no longer growing and anything that is not growing is dying. We must work on our soul, just as a gardener cultivates the soil to break up and loosening the soil in their garden. We must loosen the soul from bondages and beliefs and mental constructs that we have acquired. I refer to this as unlearning what we have learned. It is being transformed now to think as God in earth.

Cultivating breaks up the crusty soil surface allowing for a much easier penetration of air, nutrients and water deep into the soil where plant roots can gain access to them. Our souls must be cultivated, breaking up the stony heart to make it pliable to receive the Word of God, the Logos and Rhema. The Word of God that was in the beginning referenced in John 1:1-2 has always been etched upon our hearts, so that we can be useable.

The world is looking for what you have to offer, scripture says "the earth is groaning and travailing waiting for God's sons to manifest" (Romans 8:19). Son in this context is not gender specific it denotes as a spirit of maturity or mature spirit. It's time for God's son to mature, to develop our mental construct so that we can change our reality, stagger our imagination, transform our mind, shift our circumstances, restore our broken focus, bend our reality, bring definition to our identity, which brings us into our defining moment.

The Answer To My Quest

(Luke 17:21) gives us the depiction of what the kingdom looks like "neither shall they say, Lo here! or, lo there! for, behold, the kingdom of God is within you." My quest, led me to understand that the kingdom is not made by the hands of man but is within every one of us. God placed it there! Kingdom is a mindset, it is not an organization, a network nor a denomination. It is a progressive state of mental operation of the government of Heaven. Government is derived from the Latin verb Guverno, meaning "To Control" & Latin noun Mens, or Menti meaning "Mind" It is a mental construct from the divine mind of God which always existed. No one can give it to you. We are all born with this mind. However, most people are not aware that they have the mind of God within them - Fox's, have holes the birds of the field have nests but the son of man does not have place to lay his head (Matthew 8:20). The Architect of the planets and galaxies is living in us. And because He lives within…We – God sons - should never be behind, we should be the most creative and productive people on earth.

God Desires To Have Influence Through Us

The expansion in the "mind" is the expensive part of the journey. Whenever God does something, He intends to make the maximum impact. He will orchestrate events and circumstances to expand us, into the knowledge of who we are and what we are. Not everyone comprehends the opportunity when presented to expand. Mistakenly we see oppositions as trouble. We aren't in trouble, we are in transit(ion). Times of transition are set up to evaluate each of us for promotion here in earth. We are evolving (2 Corinthians 3:18) says "And we all, who with unveiled faces contemplate the Lord's glory, are being transformed into his image with ever-increasing glory, which comes from the Lord, who is the Spirit". Be grateful for every experience which called for the greatest expression in the Kingdom of your identity as God in earth.

Today We Are Finding The Term *"Kingdom"* Or *"Kingdom Minded"* Has In Some Circles Become Nothing More Than A *Buzzword*.

You can't be "kingdom" and continue to operate from a religious (to bind again) platform, embrace the religious culture or teach religious messages. You will never understand the dynamics of the kingdom with a church mindset. Many acting like they're kingdom but have not changed out the old wine skin (thoughts) for new wine skin. In the Greek theater, actors would talk or speak (krinomai) while wearing a mask (hypo). When you put these two Greek words together they form the word 'hupokris', by which we get the word hypocrisy."

Perhaps you're reading this because you're on a quest to find your place in the world. Don't stop until you see it. The greatest travesty of our day is saying we believe things we aren't seeing. Everything you see on earth has come from heaven. Gods uses the platform of the earth to deliver it to the kingdom (the mind).

- God is the "one perfect" life flowing through us.
- God is the "one Omnipresent" source at all times.
- God is the "one power" source that works inside of us.
- God is the "one pure substance" out of which our organism is formed.

God is alpha - beginning of time – omega - end of time. God created earth outside of time. That means you existed outside of time with God to see at all times at the same time. Nothing within time will cause you to lose focus, neither fret, because all will be on time. Don't be emotionally driven. You will not miss a thing. I had many hard experiences to awaken me to my truest identity hidden in God. I was who God intended for me to be already, I had to awaken to the reality of it. I had to come from the emotional roller coaster.

How Do You Get Off The Emotional Roller Coaster?

Very simply, as clearly written in (Matthew 6:25-34) "Take no thought...Why are you taking thought? Take no thought. How do we live from this place? (Genesis 12:4) records: "And Abram DEPARTD", In other words, Abram left, he did not give thought, towards what he was leaving 'behind'. He, also left his former beliefs and set his affections on things ABOVE rather then things of the earth. He had to 'come out from among them (thoughts) and be ye separate' in the reality of his identity? That is a result of our walking in who we have always been from the foundation of the world. The experience that I am describing is going from thinking that we are Abram to Abraham and from thinking that we are Sarai to Sarah. We are resonating with Spirit Breath and our divine womb has conceived from the mind of Christ while the thoughts of the carnal mind have been swallowed up; becoming one with Christ. The two have become one in our experience. We are no longer birthing out babies but a man child or full experience of Christ.

Where Is My Home

Some may say, "it is fifty million light years away, when I die, I'll experience it". My 'home' is walking by the spirit. My home is putting on the mind of Christ. My home is experiencing who I've always been. In the story of the prodigal son, he was told to go back home. (Luke 15:11-32) The prodigal son, losing it all had to return home. I was told to go back home to my father's house, after trying to fix things and make things happen. You know how we do. Especially women we want to be in control of everything. Yet, God was not referring to my natural father's house. He was saying, are you willing to become nothing to come back into wholeness? Wholeness meaning all-inclusive of everything pertaining to my life. Are you willing to become nothing to come back home to the MIND of God? When I say this, I express to you to come back to your original way of thinking. This is done by transforming our mind. To transform means to metamorphosis- 'meta' means beyond. We are to think beyond the physical or carnal plane. Each of us must endure a metamorphosis to change in form and develop the type of thinking patterns that originates from our original state of being. A change in your life will not manifest until you have a renewed mind. Carnality or a carnal mind is an acquired mental state, we aren't born to think opposite of Christ. We are living in a day and time were God's son are being overtaken by carnal thinking. A mind that is left unrenewed becomes subjugated to character assignation. A mind that is left unrenewed will kill, steal and destroy it host and its lineage.

We all must reset our mind put our mind back into original place or position. If were not watchful our carnal mind will have us misjudging what is actually happening spiritually. Our carnal mind will keep us angry at people for trying to destroy us, when in the spirit God is attempting to promote us. A carnal mind will have you beating at the wind and calling warfare what is actually God's means of evaluating each of us. An evaluation comes to determine our set value and to determine our significance. This is the reason why Jacob said to the angel "I will not let you go until you bless me". (Genesis 32:25) After evaluation comes the name change and your value changes in earth as it is in heaven. What came to destroy you is the same things that God will use to promote you and awaken you so that you can come into view from places of obscurity.

Dominate In Our Thoughts

We are created to have dominion, this includes our thought life and were not to be dominated by them. We don't have to fight for dominion, nor bind and loose for it. But you and I have been given dominion. Have denotes out of 'rest'. The fact that God said have dominion, is because He knew carnality would try to rule over you. Our suffering is caused by our mind. Our mind has preferences and will insist on us giving it what it wants. True joy comes from the person who lets their physical world flow with their spirit. We do this by shifting from fleshly thoughts to spiritual thoughts, allow the will of the Father to be done in our life. It is with this mindset that our awareness of who we are expand and what we are is defined.

Are You Willing?

My QUEST-ION for you, are you willing to become nothing to come back home? To move from carnal thinking to spiritual thinking. You are going to have to walk it alone. No one can do it for you, you must go alone. When Jacob had to finally realize he could not manipulate Esau he had to return back to his country and kindred which represents the mind of

Christ. (Genesis 31:3) Unlike the prodigal, Jacob was very rich when he came to himself but still encourage to go back to his home. As did the prodigal son, me, Jacob and many of you, are wrestling with the angel of God, in the process of returning home. Walking in the spirit and not in the flesh. Home is who you are and have always been…Home is the mind of God which you have always had…Stay on your quest.

Response:

You will turn now to Spirit within and discover the answer which has always been.

Declaration:

I decree I am returning back home to my father's house, the mind of Christ.

Session V

Conclusion

We are solely responsible for the results in our lives. Regardless of outside influences or circumstances, we can always choose what we think and what we do, and we are accountable for the results that we create because of our own choices.

The sad reality is that most people blame the ending results on someone outside of themselves. Never wanting to be held accountable. To be perceived as victim in the story hold a greater reward. We get to tell our story like a virus and spread it to everyone in our circle of influence who listens so they can protect us in our inadequacy.

Do not allow your story to become your suffering. You are an interesting creature. Such an amazing mix. You are capable of such beautiful dreams and such horrible nightmares. Do not allow your suffering to become your identity. Stop sabotaging your future; a victim mentality is a sabotaging mentality. It is easy to blame your 'ex' for the breakdown of your relationship. No! Ask yourself how did I participate in this breakdown? Yes, you were instrumental, perhaps not the starting role, however, you contributed. How you perceive it and respond to it says a lot. It is time, to take accountability for your reality!

Bonus

Day 22

Hello World It's Me _____.

Think Yourself Rich

Mankind is a thinking center, and can originate thought. All the forms that man fashions with his hands must first exist in his thought; he cannot shape a thing until he has thought that thing.

You do not want to get rich, so you can boast how successful you are or outshine others with what you have accumulated while others struggle in the midst. This will only be a temporary fix of self – gratification. The person who lives for the pleasure of what their wealth brings them emotionally will only have a partial life, and will never be satisfied with what they've acquired.

You want to get rich in order that you may live life abundantly and be happy doing it so when it is time to do these things; in order that you may surround yourself with beautiful things, see distant lands, feed your mind, and develop your intellect; in order that you may love men and do kind things, and be able to play a good part in helping the world to find truth.

KNOW that the money you need will come, even if a thousand men discover it initially. I mentor clients from all over the country, a few internationally, I often tell each client, when an idea is released from the invisible realm it does so for multiple people at the same time. Those who move out on the idea are the first partakers of the substance it produces. No one can prevent you from getting what's yours.

So never allow yourself to think for an instant that all the best trees in the forest will be taken before you get ready to build your house, unless you hurry. Never worry about the trusts and combines, and get anxious for fear they will soon come to own the whole earth. Never get afraid that you will lose what you want because some other person "steps into it first." That cannot possibly happen; you are not seeking anything that is possessed by anybody else. We are all landlords and, stewards. You are causing what you want to be created from invisible substance, and the supply is without limits.

Your Now

The "future" speaks of a dimension of time and distance. "Now" speaks of space, where you are, what's inside you and a knowing of where it is taking you. The culmination of situations that happened on your journey is because God was empowering you for your NOW!

You must vision your NOW. See with your spirit and allow it to articulate itself to you. Whatever God purposed for you to do, it's not in the future it is IN you right NOW. Although it is taking time to manifest itself to you, it is still happening right NOW!

Seven steps to manifesting your desire:

1. Vision – Visualize what you want.
2. Desire - Be intensely excited about what you've visualizing.
3. Belief – Believe what you desire is possible to manifest.
4. Acceptance – Accept your belief and your ability to manifest it as being true.
5. Intend – Want and intend are different. You must have the intention to manifest your desire.
6. Action – Act and behave like your desire has already manifested.
7. Allowance – Detach from the outcome. You have to be intense in your desire without any expected outcome.

When manifesting your desire:

1. Always stay positive.
2. Say it like its already done.
3. Do not spend time thinking about anything opposite to what you want.
4. Mediate on what you want.
5. See it, smell it, feel it, hear it and walk in it.

6. If it's real in your brain, it will be real in the physical.

Quotes

What you think of yourself is limited by your concept of God. Your concept of God is limited by the idea of how we see yourself. – Angela Y Ervin

Your Mind is the spiritual womb of conception, be mindful of who's ideal you let impregnate you. – Angela Y. Ervin

Study to show thyself approve: I do not study to be a better speaker. I study to be a better mother, a better daughter, a better sister, a better friend and a better future wife. – Angela Y. Ervin

Our creator does not need our money He needs our Mind so that He can release His creativity in earth. - Angela Y. Ervin

Too many people are too busy looking up and not enough looking within. – Angela Y. Ervin

It's not about your issues, it's about who you can help with theirs. You are here to solve a problem! – Angela Y. Ervin

Your brain is the government of your body – Angela Y. Ervin

Most people who hide in the crowd do not get remembered. – Angela Y. Ervin

You can change your life by doing the following three things. – Angela Y. Ervin

1. Change your mindset.

2. Change your relationships.

3. Change where you go.

I AM That Lady, Angela!

Appendix

Charles Fillmore

Merriam Webster

John C. Maxwell

Law of Attraction

The Washington.edu

Poet Edgar A. Guest

George Orwell quotes

National Rape Statistics

Center for Disease Control

Overcoming Miscarriage -google

John C. Maxwell 360 Degree Leader

The Ethics & Religious Liberty Commission

Dr. Michael Barry The Forgiveness Project Copyright 2015

Dr. Jonathan David Developing A Healthy Mind Copyright 1993

to Dr. Steven Standiford, chief of surgery at the Cancer Treatment Centers of America

Author Website

www.AngelaYErvin.com

Other Books by Angela Y. Ervin

The Power to Heal

Mind Benders

(Hartford, WI: Legacy Publishing, 2016)

Arise of the Female Entreprenuer

(Hartford, WI: Legacy Publishing, 2018)

Other Resources:

By Angela Y. Ervin are also available such as Personal Development Coaching & Business Coaching & 90 – Day Mentor-Ship

Please see our contact information to see a full range of resources by Angela Y. Ervin.

I would add contact email. web and phone etc....HERE

www.ingramcontent.com/pod-product-compliance
Lightning Source LLC
Chambersburg PA
CBHW070506100426
42743CB00010B/1774